Routledge Revivals

From Renaissance to Revolution

From Renaissance to Revolution (1923) traces in some of its many expressions the influence of the Renaissance on the politics and culture of Europe during the sixteenth, seventeenth and eighteenth centuries. It starts with the decay of medieval civilisation and the emergence through the Renaissance of the independent state and the individual, and goes on the analyse the Renaissance state as perfected in one form by France and in another by its rival Holland. It discusses the influence of the Renaissance on literature and culture, and estimates the intellectual freedom it achieved for the individual in politics, science and religion.

From Renaissance to Revolution

A Study of the Influence of the Renaissance upon the Political Development of Europe

Sylvia Benians

First published in 1923
by Methuen & Co. Ltd.

This edition first published in 2025 by Routledge
4 Park Square, Milton Park, Abingdon, Oxon, OX14 4RN

and by Routledge
605 Third Avenue, New York, NY 10017

Routledge is an imprint of the Taylor & Francis Group, an informa business

All rights reserved. No part of this book may be reprinted or reproduced or utilised in any form or by any electronic, mechanical, or other means, now known or hereafter invented, including photocopying and recording, or in any information storage or retrieval system, without permission in writing from the publishers.

Publisher's Note
The publisher has gone to great lengths to ensure the quality of this reprint but points out that some imperfections in the original copies may be apparent.

Disclaimer
The publisher has made every effort to trace copyright holders and welcomes correspondence from those they have been unable to contact.

A Library of Congress record exists under LCCN 24029995

ISBN: 978-1-032-90396-5 (hbk)
ISBN: 978-1-003-55778-4 (ebk)
ISBN: 978-1-032-90397-2 (pbk)

Book DOI 10.4324/9781003557784

FROM RENAISSANCE TO REVOLUTION

A STUDY OF THE INFLUENCE OF THE RENAISSANCE UPON THE POLITICAL DEVELOPMENT OF EUROPE

BY

SYLVIA BENIANS

SOMETIME SCHOLAR OF GIRTON COLLEGE, CAMBRIDGE

WITH FOUR MAPS

METHUEN & CO. LTD.
36 ESSEX STREET W.C.
LONDON

First Published in 1923

PRINTED IN GREAT BRITAIN

TO
MY FATHER
JOHN THEODORE DODD

CONTENTS

CHAPTER		PAGE
	INTRODUCTION	ix
I.	RENAISSANCE	1
II.	REFORMATION	26
III.	LEVIATHAN	50
IV.	THE SPIRIT OF MAN	77
V.	THE EXPANSION OF THE RENAISSANCE STATES	108
VI.	THE AGE OF REASON	128
VII.	REGENERATE MONARCHY	155
VIII.	CONCLUSION	179
	INDEX	201

MAPS—   AT END OF BOOK
1. EUROPE *c.* 1519
2. THE UNITED NETHERLANDS IN THE XVII CENTURY
3. EUROPE IN 1702
4. OVERSEAS POSSESSIONS OF THE EUROPEAN POWERS IN 1762

INTRODUCTION

TWO of the ideas most firmly planted in modern minds are the paramount importance of the state on the one hand, of the individual on the other. Most of the problems of to-day arise from the passionate assertion of one or other of these beliefs; but, strongly rooted as they are, their widespread cultivation is comparatively recent. In the Middle Ages they were buried seeds. They flowered in the Renaissance, and their vigorous growth in the next three hundred years persuaded the eighteenth century to look to their harvest for the Golden Age. To-day there are people who believe that many purposes for which the state exists could be better fulfilled by other institutions and that individualism permits in practice the exploitation of the weak by the strong. But though some have lost faith in the state, and others in the individual, the work of the Renaissance was so lasting that it is only the few who have ceased to believe in either.

The illimitable rights of modern states and the correspondingly narrow interpretation they put upon the duty of world-service are due not so much to the natural inclination of governments as to a slow change in the basis of Western culture. Civilization rests now upon the diversities of national states: in the Middle Ages it was based, not upon national variation, but upon Christian unity. This unity, symbolized by the universal sway of Emperor and Pope, was founded on fact,— on the broad geographical and climatic sameness of the Mediterranean area, on the spiritual unity of mankind proclaimed by the Christian faith, on the memories and remains of the world-wide culture of Rome. Apart from accepting the vague political suzerainty of the Emperor and the spiritual supremacy of the Pope, mediæval kings had a duty to Christendom which transcended their duty to their own dominions. Some rulers cared for their own countries to the neglect of Christendom, but these did not earn the loving fame given to the memory of Richard I of England and Louis IX of France, who were thought to have placed the service of the Christian commonwealth above that of their kingdoms.

Mediæval society was divided primarily not into nations, but into social and occupational groups, which had little or no relation to the divisions of kingdoms. Towns of different countries made treaties with each other without referring to their central governments. A high-born family such as that of the Les Baux in Provence would intermarry with the proudest families of Christendom, just as kings and queens might do; and while an English and Italian priest would speak the same tongue, teach the same doctrine, wear the same clothes and claim the same rights, a Suffolk villein and a north-country knight would differ entirely in language, dress, privileges and thoughts.

Again, the position and power of such groups depended partly on the duties they discharged to humanity as then conceived, not merely on their usefulness to their own members or to the kingdom that contained them. Monasteries did not exist merely to save the souls of the monks, but also to serve humanity by prayer. The gilds were not intended simply to control trade, nor to secure good conditions of labour for their members, but also to fulfil the Christian purpose of selling honest work to the public at a fair price.

INTRODUCTION   xi

What made the mediæval group differ still more from its modern successors was its relation to its members. The status and opinions of a modern man need not depend upon his membership of a particular group : of two men bred to the same trade one may become a landowning peer, the other be a landless day-labourer all his life ; one may be a Plymouth Brother and the other an Old Catholic ; one a communist, the other a Tory. To-day, in short, the individual is more important than his group. In the Middle Ages the group counted for everything, the individual for nothing.

The most lasting achievement of the Renaissance was the fundamental change its leaders began to make in the position of the individual in society. Slowly society came to be identified with the state ; more slowly still the individual claimed and won freedom from all authority save that of the king. The movement was not only practical but ethical : it transformed public opinion as well as facts. It was accepted, not only as a fact, but as the will of God, that kings should be stronger than Emperors and Popes, that thinkers should write and say what they would, that the strong should make whatever use they pleased of their gifts and opportunities, provided always that the political supremacy of the king were unimpaired.

This revolution took three centuries to mature. The old civilization died hard ; and the two main objects of Renaissance pioneers, the supremacy of the dynastic state and the freedom of the individual, were not compatible for long. And when in the eighteenth century reformers tried to fuse the two divergent aims, their efforts were frustrated by the French Revolution.

The nineteenth century was, it is true, the heyday of individualism and state sovereignty. But on the whole it seems just to regard the French Revolution as the final solvent of the civilization handed down from the Renaissance. The individual freedom aimed at in the nineteenth century was political, not simply intellectual and social; and the ideal sovereign state was a democratic and national organism, and not the dynastic and autocratically ruled administrative area desired in the century before.

The aim of the following chapters is to trace in some of its many expressions the influence of the Renaissance on the politics and culture of Europe during the sixteenth, seventeenth and eighteenth centuries. I have attempted to do this in a way that I hope may be interesting to the general reader and not without usefulness to the student of the outlines of modern history. Starting from the decay of mediæval civilization and the emergence through the Renaissance of the independent state and the independent man, I have gone on to describe the Renaissance state as perfected in one form by France and in another by her rival Holland. I have then discussed the influence of the Renaissance on literature and culture, especially in France, and have also tried to estimate the intellectual freedom it achieved for the individual in politics, science and religion. In chapter v I have outlined the different ways in which Renaissance states sought completion in oversea expansion; and in the next two chapters have described the attempt made in the eighteenth century to enlarge and combine the two Renaissance ideals of individualism and state sovereignty,—chapter vi being devoted primarily to the history of ideas, chapter vii to the legislation and policy of the Enlightened Despots. My last chapter indicates the rise of new forces which were to influence and to some extent displace the traditions of the Renaissance.

FROM RENAISSANCE
TO REVOLUTION

CHAPTER I

RENAISSANCE

> " Princes' images on their tombs do not lie, as they were wont seeming to pray up to heaven ; . . . they are not carved with their eyes fixed upon the stars ; but as their minds were wholly bent upon the world, the self-same way they seem to turn their faces."
> Webster, *Duchess of Malfi*, Act IV, Sc. ii.

> " . . . For it may truly be affirmed to the honour of these times, and in a virtuous emulation with antiquity, that this great building of the world had never through-lights made in it, till the age of us and our fathers . . . to circle the earth as the heavenly bodies do, was not done, nor enterprised till these later times."
> Bacon, *Advancement of Learning*, II, 13.

THE Renaissance was no cataclysm. Long before the close of the Middle Ages Europe was tossing restlessly ; and, on the other hand, many of the mediæval shadows were not dispelled by the dawn of the modern world. Yet it is clear that the fifteenth and sixteenth centuries were a time of abnormally swift change. It was in this era that the mental pendulum of humanity swung from vain longing for an unhistorical past to the glorification of the present by the aid of the past, from the unquestioning reverence for authority to a mistrust of all save experience. The change was not complete ; in the sphere of civil government a strong movement for state-independence was hindered by a counter-movement for universal empire ; religious independence of individuals and churches was challenged by the claim of each sect in the hour of triumph to dominate the world by persecution ; and new truths replaced old traditions only by the slow gain of painful inches. But however great the success of theologians in impressing European thought with the notion of man's vileness and helplessness, the vigour and resource, the daring and the zest for life of the Renaissance leaders, whether men of thought or men of action, were a persistent challenge to those who contemned the life of this world. Man, instead of being cowed by the visible and invisible forces at work around him, lifted his head to do battle, and began to feel with increasing assurance, whether rightly or wrongly, that he was to be master of his fate.

Criticism, humanism, and curiosity were the three great passions that gave driving force to the Renaissance, and they combined in different ways to compass three great ventures, the discovery of the old world, the discovery of the world in which they fermented, and the discovery of new worlds in space and thought.

The ancient world was never entirely lost to mediæval Europe. But a half-truth is often more misleading than a lie, and it seems probable that Greek and Roman civilization as reconstructed by mediæval thinkers would not have been recognized by the ancients themselves. Certainly Virgil could scarcely have seen himself in the far-famed magician whom the Middle Ages called by his name.

The government to which mediæval Europe looked back with so great a sense of loss was the government of imperial Rome. In an age of barbarian incursions followed by internal warfare the Pax Romana of the Antonines naturally seemed the highest ideal to which civilization could aspire, and the old creative days of the Republic would have seemed less interesting even if much had been known about them. Similarly, their interpretation of Greek thought was falsely coloured by mediæval thinkers with the needs of their own times. Plato and Aristotle, first regarded askance by the Church, were later introduced, as it were, into the Christian fold by the efforts of the schoolmen, who claimed to have harmonized Greek philosophy with Christian teaching. Again, the humanistic thought of the Greeks would have been largely lost on an age in which the scholars and teachers were clerics, who, whatever they thought in private, were supposed to regard the human body as a stumbling-block on the path of virtue, and the joys of the world as a hindrance, or at best a waste of time, on the way to heaven.

It was not only that the thought of mediæval writers was confined by the circle of ideas into which they had been born. Minds of rare independence such as that of Marsilius of Padua, who deduced the sovereignty of the people from his knowledge of Roman history and his study of Aristotle, could not have restored to the world the spirit of Greek independence and curiosity in art, philosophy and science owing to the scarcity of Greek records in mediæval Europe. It was not until the thirteenth century that the greater part of Aristotle was rediscovered, and all that the Middle Ages knew of Plato was a mere fragment of his work. Nor was their scanty knowledge of Greek for the most part gained direct, but only through translations, or translations of translations.

In Italy, it is true, a certain continuity can be traced between ancient and mediæval civilization. Possibly the gilds of Italian towns, unlike those in the rest of Europe, had a direct affinity with the *collegia* of Roman times; certainly Italians never forgot that the Eternal City lay in their midst, while the south of Italy never entirely lost its old connection with Greece. So it was natural that the main impulse to know more about the ancients should come from Italy. As early as the fourteenth century Petrarch (1304-1374) and his disciples were recovering classical Latin. Later

4 FROM RENAISSANCE TO REVOLUTION

began the hunt for classical manuscripts. Deep interest was shown by great men whenever a new manuscript was disinterred. Cardinals sent to Greece in the hope of procuring literary treasure trove; Popes were infected by the growing enthusiasm. Before the middle of the fifteenth century the Greek revival began. Then in mid-fifteenth century Constantinople fell before the Turks. Hundreds of Greek teachers were turned adrift, and with their load of precious manuscripts were welcomed by an eager Italy. From Italy the West and North took fire, but from the North, Italy borrowed a new and quicker tinder. For with the necessity of copying each manuscript by hand the new learning could spread but slowly, and the possession of books was the privilege of the wealthy alone. But three years before the downfall of the Eastern Empire, Gutenberg set up the first printing press in Mainz, and in 1474 his example was followed by Caxton in England. Italy responded in 1494 with the foundation at Venice of the Aldine Press, some of whose exquisitely bound fifteenth-century editions still survive.

Patient criticism was the key that best fitted the rusty lock of the past, though curiosity eased the turning. Without the work of those who

> " . . . settled *Hoti's* business . . .
> Properly based *Oun*—
> Gave us the doctrine of the enclitic *De*,"

who recreated Latin and Greek grammar and laboured on classical manuscripts, we should not only have remained relatively ignorant of the ancient world but should have missed most of the gains which that discovery has brought us. One of these gains was perhaps more important for early modern Europe than it seems to be for us. This was the recovery of classical Latin as a means of communication. The hard work of Petrarch and of many unknown scholars fashioned an almost perfect instrument for international correspondence and negotiation no less than for scholarship. Cicero and Tacitus could have read Petrarch's letters, but they might have found it as difficult as many of us do to understand the Latin of S. Bonaventura's secretary who lived less than a century earlier.

Another result of unwearying criticism was the first scientific exploration of the Scriptures. This was due to the recovery of Greek and later to the study of Hebrew. All through the Middle Ages the Latin version of the Scriptures, that is the Vulgate, was the one in general use. It was full of errors, but few had the ability or the daring to amend it by comparison with the more accurate Greek version of the Septuagint, while a Hebrew scholar was almost unknown. The eager search for manuscripts which followed on the close of the Middle Ages was not only pagan in temper ; men were no less keen to rediscover the Bible than to unearth Plato. In Italy, indeed, the two quests were often pursued together : Marsilio Ficino, though a staunch Christian, kept a lighted lamp before the bust of Plato, and no one thought his act incongruous. But in Northern Europe the discovery of manuscripts led almost exclusively to impassioned enquiry into the true meaning of the Bible. Erasmus, with his Greek version of the New Testament, was the great pioneer in this work. His example was followed by our own Colet who lectured on the Epistles of St. Paul, and by the University of Cambridge where Erasmus stayed.

The study of Greek and Hebrew not only revolutionized exegesis but also influenced theology and ecclesiastical organization. For the scientific questioning of accepted scriptural readings was naturally accompanied by the determination to test the authority of the Fathers and of the ecclesiastical traditions handed down by the Church. In the Middle Ages the Fathers and ecclesiastical tradition shared a triune sway with the Vulgate. In disputing this sway Renaissance scholars were attacking the dogma and position of the Church.

Inseparably connected with the recovery of the ancient world was the development of a humanistic spirit. Fourteenth- and fifteenth-century scholars were electrified by contact with the pagan mood of sustained delight or interest in all that belongs to human life. For one philosopher who had sighed of vanity, they found a thousand poems, plays, histories and works of art that revealed the glory of the world and threw back into shadow the " sic transit " of the Middle Ages. Not that all could forget the shadow. The thought of " Time's wingèd chariot hurrying near " seems to have haunted the Elizabethans for all their fullness of life. Knight and lady might hold sweet converse together in fair places, but skeleton Death was always leering at them from behind some tree, his hour-glass held triumphantly aloft.

In art there were signs of a humanistic spirit as early as the second quarter of the thirteenth century. Before the coming of the friars, almost the only subjects considered worthy of painting had been the lives and legends of Christ and the saints. Only incidentally do we get pictures of ordinary human life. If subjects were limited, technique was faulty. Little was known of perspective or anatomy. Matters were made worse by the influence of ecclesiastical uniformity and tradition. There came to be one way and one only of painting each scene from the life of each saint. To clothe some holy man in a robe of the wrong colour, to put in his hand anything except his proper symbol, to give him a face expressive of individuality instead of an impersonal and painful asceticism was almost impossible. It is, however, easy to exaggerate the lack of inspiration in mediæval art. When most people could not read, how were they to recognize the saint of their special devotion without his conventional signs and symbols ? One can call to mind, too, an occasional horse of real vigour, plants and birds drawn from careful observation, details in the scenes of some Biblical story obviously inspired by unecclesiastical facts, whether the tools of a trade, or Ruth's skirt, tucked up for gleaning but demurely covering her ankles at home. And in sculpture, leading mediæval craftsmen, especially in France, could hold their own with the best artists of any age. Speaking broadly and relatively, however, it is true that owing chiefly to the Church the Renaissance found "art made tongue-tied by authority," though some of the blame is due to the mediæval worship of the past which gave undue prestige to Byzantine models.

The life of St. Francis and his companions fired the imagination of Europe as nothing had done since the days of Christ. The Franciscan legend grew up mushroom-like ; and before conventional tradition had entombed the unconventional saint there was nothing to prevent each artist from developing his paintings in his own way. And the overwhelming popularity of St. Francis and his followers created an avid demand for pictorial representations of their story ; churches built in the Saint's honour must be decorated by scenes from his life. Thus in the hands of Giotto, Sassetta and the Della Robbias, Franciscan legend blossomed into rare flowers of the Renaissance : he who had urged the brethren to live in squalid undecorated huts was the unwitting father of the Italian renaissance in art.

But though the pictures of St. Francis show a freshness and originality as well as a reflection of the saint's keen enjoyment of natural beauty, they are not all marked by the glorification of the human body which was so essential a characteristic of most Renaissance art. In the vast spaces, silvery skies and ethereal figures of Sassetta cannot be found the tribute to physical perfection nor the exclusive attention to things seen which have marked most Western art since the Middle Ages ;—on the contrary, these pictures of the Sienese artist give a feeling of spirituality which is almost oriental. Giotto, however, was willing to falsify history in his worship of the human figure. Robust and large-limbed, his St. Francis could never have taken Poverty to wife nor have welcomed the ardent visitation of the Seraph. Giotto's St. Francis merely reflects the spirit of its author: in the days of the Renaissance few had a mind for voluntary starvation and poverty. So Botticelli and Raphael, Lippi and Da Vinci, differing widely from each other, were alike in their worship of the human form.

In the north of Europe, perhaps because Teutonic memory reached back no further than the Christian era, there was a general tendency still to give to art a religious complexion, although the individuality of the artist was escaping from the fetters of tradition and authority. Religious influences are strong upon the creative and vigorous work of Dürer (1471-1528) : if he was definitely influenced by Italian art when he crossed the Alps, at home he came willingly under the spell of Luther's personality and message. The Flemish pictures of the fifteenth century are also mainly religious in subject and feeling. There was always a certain amount of portrait painting, but far less than in Italy, while the great age of Netherlandish landscapes was the seventeenth century. This Christian and religious memory of Germany was in the end hostile to the humanistic spirit. German thought was ultimately concentrated mainly on the "attempt to reincarnate the apostolic mind," German energy found vent in issues of Church discipline and dogma; and in establishing the faith of Luther, Germany had to forfeit the humanism of Erasmus.

If in art the inspiration of the Renaissance emphasized national differences instead of the old cosmopolitanism of the Middle Ages, in literature the change was still more marked. In England, Italy and France, Renaissance writers fashioned their vulgar tongues, and thus intensified national spirit. What the Authorized Version of the Bible and North's Plutarch did for the English language was done for Italian by Machiavelli's prose. What was thus done with great success incidentally for England and Italy was done consciously and with less success for French poetry by a group of poets called the " Pléiade " of whom Ronsard and Du Bellay were the most famous. French prose was crystallized by Calvin, and the German tongue moulded by Luther, both of them products of the Renaissance in its broadest sense, though each in many ways its enemy. The English Renaissance developed comparatively late, but its blossoms and fruits were inferior to none produced elsewhere. England could show no great pictures or sculptures; she gave birth to no great religious movement. The inspiration of the Elizabethans found expression first of all in language and secondarily in song—in the prose of the Bible and Chapman's *Homer*, in the love-lyrics of Raleigh and Sidney, in the plays of Shakespeare and Marlowe, the madrigals of Dowland and Gibbons, the church-music of Byrd and Tallis. We remember now only the greatest names, but in those days ordinary folk considered it part of a gentleman's education to be able to compose a song or lyric, and as naturally as we sit down to play cards after dinner would they drop into their places for part-songs and instrumental music. Such wealth of expression is the truest mark of the Renaissance inspiration. The profusion of classical quotation and allusion was natural to the age which rediscovered Greece and Rome; the keen joy in living and delight in human beauty that fill Elizabethan literature are the counterpart of the same qualities in Italian art; above all, the comprehensive treatment and understanding of all the manifestations of human life, and even the refusal to judge and to discriminate, spring straight from the humanistic spirit.

The breadth and comprehensiveness that the English showed in literature had been shown by the Italians in their mastery of many fields of art and learning. Perhaps in no one sphere did they display the all-embracing genius of Shakespeare, but Shakespeare never tried to master the infinite variety of occupations that Leonardo da Vinci (1452-1519) made his own. "Racked with frustrate passion after the universal," Leonardo was at once painter, sculptor, poet, instrument-maker, engineer, scientist, philosopher, prophet, inventor and student of mechanics, optics and natural history. Nothing was too small, nothing too great for his scrutiny. Everything real, above all everything strange, was delightful to him. The only things he condemned were authority and pretence. "Whoever in a discussion uses authority uses not intellect but rather memory," he said, and he thought falsehood so vile "that, though it should praise the great works of God, it offends against His dignity." Other Italians mastered one or several of the fields over which Leonardo ranged. But whether it were in painting, sculpture, architecture, literature, philosophy, science or autobiography, they were one and all giving expression to a superabundant vigour of personality, just as the Elizabethans were to do in England.

The French Renaissance was different. It was concerned with form more than with content: it sprang from conscious effort more than from spontaneous impulse. Francis I collected artists and pictures as a connoisseur. French painters, poets and architects borrowed classical models, though by giving them a new form and perfection of finish they redeemed them from being copies and gave a national impress to their work. Its beauty is impressive, its dignity magnificent, but its perfection of symmetry and its

RENAISSANCE

self-contained calm have provoked many critics to call it a desertion of art for the artificial. It is this more than anything else which makes the Louvre so utterly different from Notre Dame: one is a tomb, the other a tree. Even Montaigne (1533-1592), whose good-humoured scepticism and tolerance stamp him as a child of the Renaissance, had a mind that was too quiet and tidy and gentle to match with the ardent, almost boisterous prodigality of idea and effort that marked the greatest men of the day. Yet his predecessor Rabelais (?1483-1553) was an exception. He had all the vitality of the Renaissance, all its breadth of intellectual grasp, all its distaste for the shams of a bygone age, all its zest for everything that belonged to human life. He said he disliked one thing only, and that was contempt of the commonplace. Like Shakespeare and Machiavelli, he was an artist and not a moralist, but among all the manifestations of human life that engrossed him he did single out one for pre-eminence, and that was man's capacity for laughter. It was laughter that raised man above the animals—a kindly laughter born of large-hearted charity, and untouched by cynicism.

The passionate curiosity of Leonardo was symbolic of his age. It was an age of mechanical and technical innovations. Of these new additions to Western civilization, the most revolutionary were the press, gunpowder and the compass, all alike previously invented by the Chinese. "No empire, sect, or star," wrote Bacon, "appears to have exercised a greater power or influence on human affairs than these mechanical discoveries."[1] Decisive technical advances were made also in map-drawing and the laws of perspective. But in pure thought, the fruits of intellectual curiosity were small and scanty in the fifteenth and sixteenth centuries. It seems as though thinkers were too much dazzled by their discovery of ancient thought to be

[1] Quoted Bury, *The Idea of Progress*, p. 54.

able to seek beyond the achievements of Greece and Rome. The supremacy of Greek thought in medicine and astronomy was threatened, but though Copernicus affirmed (*c.* 1530) the falsity of the old geocentric astronomy, few believed him; and when, in the next century, Galileo proved that Copernicus was right, he was put in prison. Bacon himself did not accept their conclusions. Belief in astrology and witchcraft was widespread all through the Renaissance period. The main achievement in the sphere of thought was rather a change of attitude than any definite physical discovery or philosophical achievement. Out of the Renaissance came that distrust for authority and that patience which is content to wait for generalizations till facts are examined, without which modern science and modern philosophy would have been impossible.

On the other hand, geographical discoveries of the first importance were the result of a less purely intellectual curiosity which added new worlds to old. It is almost impossible to overestimate the results of removing the old horizon of the world. The knowledge of the New World and the penetration of the Far East were the final solvent of the old mediæval unity. In 1522 Magellan's ship came home after circumnavigating the globe. Europe was convicted of being a fraction of the earth's immensity; her civilization and culture proved to be but one among many others of longer ancestry. The political and economic centre of gravity within Europe, too, was ultimately shifted by the new discoveries. Civilization had been Mediterranean since Roman times: it now started to become Atlantic. Throughout the Middle Ages the main centres of activity had been Italy, Germany and France, while Iberia, the British Isles and Scandinavia made a more barbarous circumference. Cut off from the Mediterranean on the one hand, forced to compete with Germany and the Netherlands for the Baltic trade on the other, mediæval England had had a poor commercial outlook. After the Renaissance, England and Spain, the outposts of Europe but the stepping-stones between the Old and New Worlds, became the centres of Western activities. Italy and Germany, owing partly to a less favourable geographical position, but still more to their want of political cohesion, could gain little by the new discoveries; France, though well situated and more united, was handicapped through the greater part of the sixteenth century by the stress of civil war. Austria was geographically remote and politically detached because of her internal religious troubles and her continued struggle with the Turks. So the great political drama of the sixteenth century was played out by England and Spain. In view of the later triumph of England over both Spain and France, it is interesting to remember that after the loss of Calais England had an oceanic orientation, while Spain and France, who met in Italy, were always distracted by Mediterranean politics.

Trade was both the parent and the child of the New World. It was largely owing to the needs of trade that the efforts were made which discovered America; and on the other hand it was the discovery of the Americas that enhanced both the volume and activity of trade. Here again is a key to the history that followed: most of the wars of the Middle Ages and indeed of the Renaissance itself were religious wars, but already in sixteenth-century wars religious zeal was often the cloak of commercial rivalry, and once the most violent effects of the Reformation were spent, the era of trade wars began.

But the growth of trade not only promoted rivalry in war and shipbuilding: it had another important result in stimulating new forms of co-operation for profit among the merchants who adventured and the people who stayed at home. During the Middle Ages companies of various kinds had existed, especially among the Italians, but the usury prohibitions had to some extent hindered their growth, and the trading impulse was not strong enough to achieve a general development in this line. By the emancipated thought of the Renaissance, however, above all by the quickened stimulus due to the importation of strange and rare delights and the stories of yet rarer and more marvellous products abroad, and by the existence of capital wherewith to furnish expeditions, the way was paved for the creation of new companies and for reorganizing the old ones.

But it is easy to antedate the economic changes which followed the great discoveries. Elizabeth's England was still a small nation unconscious of its imperial destiny; the great age of companies was the seventeenth century; and not until the eighteenth century did the Atlantic trade rival in bulk the trade of the Baltic. The sixteenth century could discover, but it had the less time to organize.

It had, however, time to think. When the ancient world had been discovered and while the new world was being added to the old, the children of the Renaissance might have wept for new worlds to conquer. But thinkers sat down and created new worlds of their own out of the inspirations that were given to them by the discovery of an old world of time and a new world of space. And, as if they were inspired more by the discovery of the new world than by the recovery of the old, they put their Utopias, not in the past, nor yet in the future, but in some undiscovered place.[1]

The success of the Renaissance was ensured when its leaders captured the great powers of Church and State. Kings and queens and princesses courted artists and thinkers and gave them a living. Neither schools nor universities, but the courts, were the foster-parents of the new learning and the new art and the new politics. In spirit the Renaissance

[1] Bury, *The Idea of Progress*, p. 61.

was hostile to the Church, but the Papacy did not understand that at first, and one Pope after another gave the sanction of Christendom to the firstfruits of the movement. They rivalled the kings not only in patronizing artists and collecting treasures of every kind but in transforming the Papal States as far as they could into a Renaissance despotism.

Yet the Renaissance did more for monarchy than monarchy did for the Renaissance. Intellectually, it is true, the dominant note of the fifteenth and sixteenth centuries was liberty and not authority. But just as the most usual result of revolution is to substitute one authority for another, so in almost every direction the Renaissance was to lay down new rules in the place of the old ones which it swept away. And in no sphere was this process so complete or so rapid as in the sphere of politics.

In politics, it is true, the work of the Renaissance was not pre-eminently creative. All it did was to crystallize and justify a development already strong in the fifteenth century—the growth of kingly power and the maintenance of state independence.

When the impotence of the Holy Roman Empire and the contraction of Papal power had destroyed the political vision of the Middle Ages, the ideal of a united Christendom was replaced by the conflicting ambitions of dynastic states. The change did not mean simply that dynastic ambitions grew stronger as Church and Empire grew weaker, but that public opinion deserted the cause of Christendom for that of a royal family.

Though by the close of the thirteenth century the question was not whether, but when, Europe would break up into a number of independent states, it was not so clear that the typical government of these emerging states would be an absolute monarchy, nor that its ideal basis would be a nation. Why should it not have been a baronial oligarchy, why not a congeries of petty republics or tyrannies, why not a quasi-federal organization like that of Switzerland, why not a collection of territories with no racial unity, but inherited or conquered, like the Burgundian state which Charles the Bold only just failed to create? Fifteenth-century Europe contained at least one example of all these different types of state, but the states in which the decay of local loyalties was accompanied by the persevering and deliberate efforts of the crown grew stronger and more prosperous than others, and so their governments excited the emulation of foreigners and the approval of their own subjects.

In Tudor times the monarchies of England, France and Spain were nearing the long-sought goal of territorial unification. The French monarchy incorporated Brittany, Burgundy, Orleans, Maine, Blois and Provence in the reigns of Louis XI and Louis XII. Ferdinand and Isabella united by their marriage the two greatest kingdoms of Spain, and conquered the southern part of the peninsula from the Moors. The Tudors incorporated Wales with England, and made a serious attempt to govern Ireland. They succeeded earlier than the French or Spanish kings in seriously weakening the power of the nobility. They came nearer to realizing the autocratic ideal of administration by a nobility of service and by prerogative courts where the king's word was law. But the French kings, though they could not deprive the nobility of power, gave no encouragement to the development of constitutional government. And Ferdinand and Isabella tried to govern the whole of Spain by the autocratic methods they used in Castile.

All three powers made good their claims against Papal interference; England by throwing off all connection with Rome, and France by preserving the degree of independence won by her thirteenth-century kings and by the Gallican Church in the fifteenth century. Spain was more wholeheartedly in sympathy with the Roman faith than any other nation, but that did not prevent her kings from keeping the Pope at arm's length whenever he threatened to weaken their control over their dominions.

The kings did not owe their success to perseverance alone. The decay of mediæval institutions led to a divorce between power and social service that made the lower classes look to the king instead of to Church or baronage. It led also to the growth of a middle class who not only wanted internal peace for the sake of wealth, but who, because they were rich, could afford to lend money to the king. This enabled him more and more to dispense with the feudal administrative system without which, in the Middle Ages, government could not have been carried on for a single day.

Again, as local loyalties decayed and the imperial bond wore thin, a spirit of national pride emerged and centred its hopes in the crown. Unified territory and centralized administration were wanted by the kings for power, and by the peoples for peace and national pride. Strong monarchy in France and England thus became a vital part of the national being, not merely its outer garment. In Spain, where national pride did not seek political unity, monarchy was never more than a cloak or mask which did not fit.

The Renaissance increased the royal power in many ways. Geographical discoveries increased the volume of trade which enriched both the kings and the middle classes who supported them. National pride, which served the cause of monarchy, was fortified by the crystallization and use of the vernaculars. Two of the new inventions were still more helpful. Gunpowder made feudal warfare obsolete: the press lightened the difficulties of centralized administration. Finally, Renaissance thinkers strengthened absolute monarchy by treating it, not simply as a fact, but also as a useful fact, and in later times as an ideal.

18 FROM RENAISSANCE TO REVOLUTION

The praise of monarchy came partly from the study of the past. The influence of Roman law, which in the late twelfth century had strengthened the Church and later the kings, was increased by the classical researches of the Renaissance. In the fifteenth and sixteenth centuries the political uses of antiquity were absolutist, probably because autocracy was on the whole popular, as well as because more was known about the Roman Empire than about the Republic. It was not until the seventeenth century, when the interests of kings were more clearly opposed to the needs of their subjects, that political thinkers delved in republican history for theories hostile to absolute rule.

Machiavelli (1469-1527) is the best known of the thinkers who analysed autocracy and supported it as a useful institution. But it is more difficult to grasp the significance of his politics than to understand the far less simple political theory of many another writer. This is partly because his precepts have become the commonplaces of international affairs, so that instead of standing out against our political background, they melt into it; and partly because he never tried to make a coherent philosophy of the state. *The Prince* is simply a handbook of useful and ill-arranged hints for the ruler who wishes to make his state secure. Machiavelli's purpose was even narrower than this, for Italy was the only state whose security he had in mind. He set out the means by which, from his opinion of human nature, his knowledge of history, his experience and observation of contemporary politics, he judged that Italy could be transformed from an arena of fighting principalities and foreign intrigues into a united, safe and free state.

It seems he meant originally to say more for nationality than for monarchy. He started as a republican, but probably the need of a patron after the fall of the republican government of Florence, and a feeling that democracy was inefficient, decided him to turn absolutist. He saw that his country's great need, like that of Greece long ago, was political stability. In his day Italy was the light of the world, but that light burned in what Dante had called " a hostelry of pain." Large states like Venice and Florence quarrelled with each other and innumerable small states; and from the thirteenth century onwards each side was ready to call in the aid of foreign rulers. No sooner were the Holy Roman Emperor and his Germans excluded than French and Spaniards vied with each other for centuries in a struggle to obtain and hold Italian principalities. In spite of Machiavelli's bad name, his central plea, upon which all his other arguments depend, is one with which the twentieth century pretends to be in sympathy, the plea of national self-determination.

Italian independence could be won, in Machiavelli's view, only by the subordination of the individual, Prince and subject alike, to this purpose. All other ends, whether selfish or ideal, were irrelevant. Here he gave the lie to the mediæval ideals of other-worldliness and united Christian endeavour. Within the state there were to be only two political classes, the ruler and the ruled. The ruler must be supreme, but in the interests of the state he must know when to renounce common morality even to the loss of personal glory. The people must obey the ruler and defend the state. The different groups, so important in the mediæval state, were to have no political power, for the government was to be carried on if possible by a bureaucracy dependent on the Prince, and not by a feudal aristocracy. Machiavelli had naturally nothing to say for the mediæval " communitas communitatum," for the small political groups in Italy had stifled the larger unit that should have contained them.

In no less startling contrast to the theory of the Middle Ages was the international position to be filled by Machiavelli's state. Italy was to be an independent state set over against other independent states. This was the denial of an all-embracing Christendom, and of the "extra-territorial" claims of Church and Empire. Neither did his political experiences allow him to think of nations as a society of friends. Italy would be surrounded by enemies. Therefore the state must be military. The Prince must be above all things a soldier. He must no longer rely on mercenary troops who "are ready enough to be your soldiers whilst you do not make war"[1] and who were often employed by Italian potentates to the ruin of their country. Instead, he must rely on a citizen army like that of the Swiss.

This reiterated stress on the military nature of the independent state had its necessary echo in Machiavelli's conception of law. It followed from the main purpose of *The Prince*, that law must be, not what abstract justice or religion might dictate, but what was most useful to the nation. But no law could be useful unless backed by military force. On the other hand, when the state is kept secure by force, good laws are the natural result. "The chief foundations of all states . . . are good laws and good arms; and as there cannot be good laws where the state is not well armed, it follows that where they are well armed they have good laws. I shall leave the laws out of the discussion and shall speak of the arms."[2] Which he does at great length.

Machiavelli's statecraft implicitly refuted mediæval ideals, but it was founded on early sixteenth-century facts. His political teaching was a synthesis of all the elements of efficiency that he saw in the most successful governments of the day. Ferdinand of Aragon was crafty and unscrupulous, but he was a successful ruler. Therefore the Prince should know how to be unscrupulous if necessity of state requires.

[1] *The Prince*, p. 98 (Everyman's Lib. Edit.).
[2] *Ib.*, p. 97.

In his preoccupation with what is, instead of with what ought to be, Machiavelli denied the Middle Ages once more, and showed himself a true son of the Renaissance. "Gratias agamus," said Bacon, "Machiavello et hujus modi scriptoribus qui aperte et indissimulanter proferunt non quid homines facere debeant sed quid faciant."[1] He was like the scientist who says that the fittest survive and the weakest die out; not like the philosophic disciple of Nietzsche who says that they ought to die out. When he advocated severe punishments he did so not on ethical grounds, but for the purely utilitarian reason that the sufferers would not be able to avenge themselves. This utilitarian spirit was, however, unscientific. Machiavelli was never interested in facts for their own sake, but only for the service they might lend to his particular purpose of national independence.

He was unscientific and alien to the Renaissance, too, in his assumption of the evil nature of man. Men "are ungrateful, fickle, false, cowards, covetous."[2] He had an eye for human weakness, and could transfix it unerringly on a pointed sentence. "When death is far distant they all wish to die for him."[3] So he measures the devotion of a people to their prince. Truer still is the contention that "men more quickly forget the death of their father than the loss of their patrimony."[4] All the same, he urges, bad as people are, they have their prejudices about right and wrong. And for security in adversity the Prince must have the people on his side. This is why right and wrong do have to be considered in statecraft; otherwise they would be irrelevant. But as people judge everything by appearances, it is the appearance and not the practice of justice and right that matters most. Let the Prince appear to be just if he can, but he should always remember that the sovereign justification in the eyes

---

[1] *History*, July, 1920, p. 85. [2] *The Prince*, p. 134.
[3] *Ib.*, p. 82. [4] *Ib.*, p. 135.

of men is success : " as long as you succeed they are yours entirely." [1]

Machiavelli's name has been handed down to execration for three reasons. In the first place his honesty, though praised by Bacon, was against him in the long run. Those who dispassionately lay bare the more ugly foundations of civilization, and who build upon them openly and unashamed or advise others to do so, are never popular with the majority, who indeed build upon the same unsightly base, but pretend they cannot see it. Secondly, Machiavelli is condemned for his deliberate perversion of morality. In actual fact he was not interested in morality save where it touched the efficiency of his state, but because he said that wickedness was sometimes expedient, which is true, he has been accused of saying, " Evil, be thou my good." On the contrary, he said that though infamy may bring empire it could never give glory. Neither did he say that might is right. He said it was useful, which is perfectly true. Thirdly, and perhaps most important, Machiavellian precepts proved so true and useful that they have controlled the everyday life of international affairs, and have too often stifled the still small voice of International Law. But it was not Machiavelli's fault that the statesmen of later ages should use for the world's daily food the bitter medicine he prescribed for Italy's disease.

If Machiavelli can be justly condemned it is for his low and narrow estimate of human nature—accurate in every detail, but by its omissions a travesty of the truth. Machiavelli's men are too vile to be ends in themselves, they are at best but instruments to the higher purpose of the state.

Renaissance thought, therefore, nourished on the facts that Machiavelli had observed, attributed to each state " the keen unpassioned beauty of a great machine." Each part of a machine has its special

[1] *The Prince*, p. 134.

function, but none is more essential than another : all alike must obey the master-hand of the mechanic. Thus in a state, aristocracy, clergy, and soldiers have their special functions, but all are equally bound to obey the master hand of the monarch. There is no room here for a feudal contract between suzerain and baronage; no conception of the king as father of his people. There are but two classes of people—the ruler and the ruled ; and but two classes of obligation, to keep order, and to obey. When Luther had given a sanction to Machiavelli's utilitarianism, a new authority was raised above individual freedom, an authority whose little finger was thicker than the loins of the mediæval empire.

The absence of political liberty was scarcely compensated by the gain of intellectual freedom, not only because despotism and free thought consorted ill together, but because the intellectual gains of the Renaissance were enjoyed by the few. It was the elect of brain, birth, opportunity and wealth who received full measure, but it may be fairly questioned whether the bulk of those who enjoyed neither wealth, leisure, genius nor good birth profited at all.

It is true that in England the Tudor monarchy did to some extent benefit all classes. The increased security that gave the rich their great houses led to an improved administration of justice; and the development of the Poor Law, finally driven into a humanitarian channel, probably brought a better chance of relief to the pauper and unemployed than had been afforded by the decayed monastic system. On the continent, however, owing largely to the persistence of internal warfare, it seems safe to say that except in the Netherlands, the poor derived no benefit from the Renaissance. And the whole of Europe was adversely affected by the rise of prices, which, though very marked in the early part of the sixteenth century, was enhanced by the influx of precious metals due to the discovery of gold and silver mines. If the increase of trade gave opportunities to many poor men of intellect and resource, these were the elect of brain. The same observation is true of the scholastic achievement of the age. Many a poor scholar rose to fame, but he owed his success to the gift of a great intellect. The poor man of average intelligence could not share in the intellectual awakening of the age : he had not sufficient education to enable him to profit by the opportunities afforded to the rich. There were indeed two innovations which would certainly have enlarged the intellectual field of average men had there been any systematic attempt to diffuse the art of reading. The invention of printing lowered the cost and raised the number of books, and the translations of the Bible into the different vernaculars made the stories and wisdom of the Scriptures accessible to all who could read. But how many people could read ?

It seems clear that there was not even a desire to give increased opportunities and interests to humanity at large. Both in ideal and in fact the civilization produced by the Renaissance was selective and aristocratic : it was not until the eighteenth century that a real if incomplete attempt was made to share the fruits of civilization with people of average intelligence and opportunity.

The brilliance of Renaissance civilization seems tarnished, too, by the darkness and oblivion to which it consigned the achievements of the Middle Ages. In the joy of discovering the new world and the old, the mediæval world was deliberately lost. The great ideal of a supreme polity of unity founded on diversity, represented for the Middle Ages by the theocracy of Church and Empire resting on occupational groups, was replaced by the Machiavellian ideal of state-right on the one hand, and by a perverted ideal of universal empire on the other. The ideal which envisaged service as the condition of power was slowly but surely abandoned for the sanction of individualistic enterprise restrained by nothing but opportunity. And though in the Middle Ages the gulf between aspiration and achievement was uncomfortably wide, the remedy was not to reduce the ideal to the level of the actual. To-day there are people who ask whether it is not possible to use the material and intellectual achievements developed from the work of Renaissance thinkers and explorers in order to recapture the best ideals of the Middle Ages without falling a prey to their worst practices. But such a question was never asked until the civilization that Europe inherited from the Renaissance had passed under the guillotine of revolutionary France.

CHAPTER II

REFORMATION

"As there were many Reformers, so likewise many Reformations; every country proceeding in a particular way and method, according as their national interest together with their constitution and clime inclined them; some angrily and with extremity; others calmly and with mediocrity. . . ."
Sir T. Browne, Religio Medici.

"So kan die Seele allis Dings emperen, on des Worts Gottis, und on das Wort Gottis ist ihr mit keinem Ding beholfen. Wo sie aber das Wort hat, so darf sie auch keines andern Dings mehr, sondern sie hat in dem Wort Gnügde: Speis, Freud, Frid, Licht, Kunst, Gerechtickeit, Warheit, Weisheit, Freiheit und allis Gut überschwenglich."
Luther, Von der Freiheit eines Christenmenchen, 1520.
(Ed. Neubauer, 1913).

FROM within and from without, in the fat years of triumph and in the lean years of reverse, the deafness of the mediæval Papacy had been assailed by the cry "Reform thyself." Once in a while, a strong Pope like Innocent III would unstop his ears and devote his energy to taking away the Church's reproach, but after his death the cry would be renewed tenfold. And when we consider the abuses of the ecclesiastical system and the strength of the forces hostile to it, we feel surprised, not that there was a Reformation, but that it did not come much earlier than the sixteenth century. Two circumstances postponed it.

One was the policy of those most anxious for reform. They concentrated their attacks on the tangible abuses of the ecclesiastical system and

REFORMATION

left Church dogma inviolate. They did not see that the system was a result of the dogma, and that real reform could therefore be achieved only by alterations of dogma.[1] Neither did they agree on the best method of reforming abuses. Some thought the Pope should have greater power; that corruption and maladministration would be minimized if more complete centralization of government and stricter supervision were introduced. Others thought that the Pope had too much power.

The second circumstance was papal policy. Most of the Popes did not want radical reform. They knew it would weaken their power and influence. They were clever enough to turn to their own purposes the two most powerful orthodox movements which might have led to reform. The first of these movements, the growth of the Mendicant Orders, was spiritual in character; the second of them, the Conciliar experiment, was constitutional. Of each the Papacy sucked the strength and perverted the ideal.

The Franciscan inspiration, though essentially orthodox and faithful to Rome, had a lay origin. Because of this unsacerdotal beginning and because of the contrast between the life of the friars and the life of the ecclesiastics, the Franciscans might unwittingly have given strength and direction to the growing religious discontent of their time. The Popes feared this. But taking advantage of the humility of St. Francis and his early companions, they were able to exploit the Franciscan ideal of Gospel life. They slowly forced the free brotherhood into the straitwaistcoat of three distinct Orders, and stereotyped the variety of Franciscan expression and adventure by imposing innumerable rules, restrictions and privileges. To gain more complete control over the Order the Papacy betrayed St. Francis by pronouncing that his last and most solemn injunctions to his friars were not

[1] *Camb. Mod. Hist.*, I, chap. xix.

28 FROM RENAISSANCE TO REVOLUTION

binding on them.[1] So the Papacy has to bear the chief responsibility for the long and bitter struggle between those Franciscans who tried to be faithful to their saint and those who preferred to obey the Pope. But the Papacy had gained incalculable moral prestige from the movement. The love and reverence which St. Francis and his followers had inspired all over Europe were garnered in the first instance [2] by the Church; at the feet of the Church fell the crown of the preachers who won the universities and the towns from the heretics, of the missionaries and martyrs who carried the faith beyond the edge of the mediæval world. From the Dominicans, it is true, the Papacy won strength more fairly. Founded by a Regular Canon with the definite aim of fighting heresy, the Order had a more definitely ecclesiastical origin than the Franciscan brotherhood, and was thus better fitted from the start for papal direction and control.

Unlike the Franciscans, the promotors of the Conciliar movement had a policy of ecclesiastical reform. They held that the evils of the Church were largely due to its autocratic form of government. They wanted a constitutional government. This desire was widely felt in the early fifteenth century, that is just before the Renaissance despots had established their positions. An attempt to gain an advanced type of constitutional government had been made in England; in Spain the Cortes of Aragon maintained a strict control over the government; in France the first States General had been called by Philip IV as early as 1302.

In the ecclesiastical polity, constitutional ideas had never been lost sight of. Theoretically a General Council was always allowed to be the supreme voice in Christendom, and in the fifteenth century it seemed to

---

[1] A moral betrayal, though legally the Pope had power to do this.

[2] When the Order split, part of it joined the Emperor against the Pope, but this was not till the fourteenth century.

many that, if this theory were put into practice, the reform of the Church " in head and members " would be assured.

But though in theory a General Council consisted of the whole people of Christendom (Ockham thought it should include women), it was an aristocratic rather than a democratic gathering which assembled at Constance in 1414. Bishops and secular princes, cardinals, abbots, knights and priests were present in large numbers, but the ordinary parish priest had no vote. The Pope was not long in showing how much reform the Conciliar Fathers might expect from him. In the first place, he had managed to delay the meeting of the Council. When he could prevent that no longer, he tried to ensure that his friends, the Italian clergy, numerically superior to the representatives of other nations, should have the controlling voice. He failed in this, but he succeeded in putting off the evil day of discussing the reform of the Church in head and members, and he took good care to profit by the disagreements of the would-be reformers. The most enthusiastic of these at the start was the Emperor Sigismund, but political troubles at home finally made him weak-kneed and inclined him to see that there was something on the Pope's side of the question. Consequently the Emperor threw away the last chance of raising imperial prestige at the expense of the Papacy, though his hands might in any case have been tied by the jealous Fathers, who were apt to regard secular help as unwarrantable interference. So much the better for the Pope. In addition, national animosities divided the would-be reformers. Worse still, the bishops soon showed that they wanted to strengthen their own position against the Pope far more keenly than they wanted Church reform : Church reform became a secondary aim with the doctors of theology, too, because they were afraid the bishops would become too strong. So it was not wonderful that in the end the only material concession wrung from the Pope was the decree "*Frequens*," a document providing for the meeting of periodic General Councils. On the other hand he had gained the condemnation and execution of the heretic Hus, and he had staved off the menace to reform the Church. Other Councils did meet, but the Popes assumed towards them an increasingly dictatorial manner. Thus, on the whole, the Papacy shook itself triumphantly free from the Conciliar ordeal. Just as Edward IV laid the ghost of the Lancastrian experiment, as Louis XI and Ferdinand of Aragon exorcised the incipient constitutionalism of their kingdoms, so did Eugenius IV escape from the toils of the Conciliar Movement and turn its failure to the profit of the Papacy. The Church was not to escape her Renaissance prince, any more than she could avoid Renaissance criticism.

If the Papacy had been both strong and undivided in purpose, the Reformation might have been staved off longer. But between 1420 and 1520 there was no Pope strong enough to take full advantage of his position. But though unable to prevent the Reformation, the Papacy might still have been able to control its course. The old tradition of Catholicism was still strong. The new intellectual movement did not at first seem hostile. Rome, though inferior to other Italian cities in creative art and thought, was in a sense the focus of the Renaissance, for under the patronage of the Papal Court the Eternal City became the change-house of the new ideas. As late as the sixteenth century many reformers believed in the possibility of reconciling the old learning and the new. Erasmus and Colet and More proved by their own life and works that the most scholarly and most spiritual of men could still cling to both. In addition there was a Catholic middle party whose strength made reconciliation seem possible until as late as 1541. Probably the Popes, if they had honestly desired reform, could have controlled this party. But the chief interest of papal policy was not reform, but the consolidation of temporal power.

This secular policy of the Papacy had long combined with the moral and financial abuses of the ecclesiastical system to alienate public opinion from the Church. By the early sixteenth century financial extortions roused especial hostility. They violated people's moral sense. They were resented on national grounds. And just as in later days the French peasants were to resent the privileges of the Seigneurs who did nothing in return for the dues they exacted, just as many people to-day think it unfair that landlords should grow rich from urban ground rents without doing any useful work, so in the Middle Ages there were many who felt the papal exactions to be unjust because nothing was received for what was paid. This accumulation of discontent with the Church was dangerously powerful. But it was purely destructive. It had nothing to put in the place of the organization it threatened. Nationality could replace the political functions of the Empire, but it was not ready in most countries to assume the spiritual duties and privileges of the Church.

The creative force of the Reformation came from the Renaissance. In a sense the Reformation was the Renaissance; it was the German Renaissance. It began in the Renaissance search for truth, it continued in the Renaissance doubt of authority. It had roots in literary criticism and in the movement for spiritual liberty. Literary criticism had proved the inaccuracy of the Vulgate by the study of Greek and Hebrew Biblical texts. A new way of finding God's meaning had been discovered: the Pope was no longer unquestioned interpreter of the Scriptures. The authority of Church tradition was thus disputed.

The movement for spiritual liberty was hostile not only to Church tradition, but to Church government and dogma. The mediæval Church had never taught that the individual is not directly responsible to God, but the excessive development of ceremonial and the enhancement of the priestly office had in practice raised a step-ladder between each man's soul and God. Another kind of step-ladder had been raised by emphasizing external means of salvation. The orthodox Roman Catholic, though always admitting the necessity of individual faith and love, had relied to a great extent on gaining the favour of God by the mediation of saints and martyrs, by the priestcraft of the hierarchy and by the efficacy of good works. But just as the reformer relied on his own interpretation of the Scriptures, so he sought salvation from within—from the gift of divine grace to his individual soul, and from the intensity of his own faith in divine goodness and mercy. It is easy to see how the conviction that true religion is a relation which each soul can establish between God and itself would take the life out of Catholic organization and teaching. If each man is his own priest, what is the function of hierarchy and sacraments? If each man must save himself with God's help alone, how can his sin be remitted by the payment of money? Even the mediation of saints is of no avail. The pronouncement of a Pope cannot be suffered to override the conviction of a single conscience.[1]

The fundamental difference between Protestantism and mediæval Catholicism is perhaps explained most simply by the difference between the mediæval and Renaissance views of the individual. In the Middle Ages, association was the means through which every purpose was fulfilled. A man's purpose to come nearer God was best fulfilled through the ritual and personnel of a society, the Church. A man's sins were forgiven him through his membership of the great society of believers, both quick and dead. His sins were cancelled as it were by a draft on the store of good

[1] So Luther held.

works, the "treasury of merits," accumulated in heaven by saints and good men, not solely for their own benefit, nor simply for the glory of God, but also for the use of distressed members of their society. In theory, at all events, the supreme arbiter in theological and ecclesiastical questions was not the Pope, an individual, but the society of a General Council. The Renaissance conception of the powers and privileges of the individual naturally brought with it the notion of individual responsibilities and duties. Even a General Council is not infallible.[1] No society can wipe out a single fault of any one man. Only God can do that. Even God cannot do it without faith on the part of the man. Without faith there is no relation between God and man. Without faith there can be no grace.

The difference between the old faith and the new was political as well as religious. The old faith fitted into the unity of Christendom: the new faith moulded and was moulded by the new force of nationality. In each land the Reformation became something distinct, and it helped to create something national. In England and Sweden it helped to create the monarchy, in Germany the kingdoms, in the Netherlands a new state. Even the opposition to the Reformation was national. The Counter-Reformation was the supreme national work of Spain.

So, thanks to the Renaissance, those who demanded reform had at last a constructive faith to offer in return for the faith they attacked. In the printing press they had an instrument for bringing their faith to many people and many lands. Above all they had men who could lead them.

The chasm between old and new was spanned by Erasmus (? 1466-1536). He did not understand the force of nationality because his country was not yet a nation. As counsellor to Charles V he was an official of the Holy Roman Empire. All his life he was a

[1] Luther.

member of the cosmopolitan society of scholars who spoke one tongue, but who were beginning in his day to break up into national groups. The paganism of the Italian Renaissance repelled him. Theology was still for him the queen of sciences. He based his own work upon the mediæval foundation of patristic writings and scholastic learning. The organization of the Church, no less than its intellectual heritage, seemed essential to him if religion were to be brought into practical life. Above all, he relied in the last resort upon authority rather than upon individual reason: he speaks of the "inviolable authority of Holy Scripture and of the Church, to which I willingly submit my reason in all things, whether I understand what it prescribes or do not understand."[1] In all this he belonged to the Middle Ages. But his passion for learning, his acute critical faculty and use of the new methods of study, his ideals of education and his hostility to old prejudice and abuse prove him a child of the Renaissance. "Determined to master this Greek"[2] in early life, he determined later to master the methods and subject matter of scholastic philosophy so that he could criticize current theological teaching. For by the time of Erasmus, scholasticism had degenerated into hair-splitting arguments no longer new, no longer interesting and with no bearing whatever upon the problems of life. He said that its leaders had the dullest intellects and most brutal manners he had ever come across.[3] He exposed their methods again and again. One "learned" friar, he says, "discovered the properties of Christ in the letters of the word Jesus. The three inflexions exhibited the triple nature—Jesus, Jesum, Jesu. That is Summus, medius, ultimus . . . They (the theologians) have their syllogisms, their majors and minors, inferences, corollaries, supposi-

---

[1] *Eng. Hist. Rev.*, Jan., 1920, p. 22.
[2] J. A. Froude, *Life and Letters of Erasmus*, p. 68.
[3] J. A. Froude, op. cit., p. 75.

tions; and, for a fifth act of the play, they tell some absurd story and interpret it allegorically, tropologically, anagogically, and make it into a chimera more extravagant than poet ever invented." No wonder " the world was sick of teaching which gave it nothing but glosses and formulas, and was thirsting after the water of life from the Gospels and Epistles."[1]

Modern in his critical faculty, he was modern too in his conception of education. "The important thing for you," he wrote to a student at Lübeck, " is not how much you know, but the quality of what you know." We have not yet improved upon that.

But Erasmus was not one of those who are torn in two by wavering sympathy with opposite extremes. He had a definite position of his own. What stood in the way of Christianity, in his opinion, was neither Popes nor indulgences nor even friars, but ignorance. Ignorance was the false foundation of sand : it must be replaced by the bed-rock of sound learning if the Church were to stand firm. His life-work was to lay the stones of this firm foundation. Both his position and his work are summed up in his New Testament. To a carefully edited Greek text he added a Latin translation. Side by side with Gospel precept he placed trenchant comments on the abuses of the Church. On such lines he hoped that " good letters " would bring about the renewal of Christendom. All parties must give up something, but the Pope would be the best leader of the reform movement. If the revolutionary methods of Luther were adopted, " good letters" might perish in the turmoil, and with them would be lost not only the best chance of reform but all that was most desirable in civilization. He told Campeggio that he " would rather see things left as they are than see a revolution which may lead to one knows not what."

The teaching of some of Luther's followers made him

[1] Erasmus to Campeggio, 1520, *ib.*, p. 277.

uneasy. "What was the use," he asked, "of telling foolish lads that the Pope is Antichrist, that confession carries the plague . . . that good works and merits are a vain imagination, that free will is an illusion?"[1] This was the sort of teaching he had opposed in the friars—teaching that flourished on the ignorance which gave it birth.

But in spite of his great reputation, Erasmus did not command a large following. He complained that he was waging a threefold war " with these Roman pagans who are jealous of me, with certain theologians and monks who are turning every stone to destroy me, and with some rabid Lutherans who roar at me because it is I alone, they say, who stay their victory."[2] A cause founded on educational ideals is seldom understood and never popular.

Luther's reform movement gained wider support. He attracted to him all the elements of discontent, whether social, religious or political, that were seething in the Empire. For a while he seemed to symbolize German nationalism; then to offer a remedy for the social grievances of the peasants. On the other hand the princes sympathized with him because his opposition to the purchase of indulgences coincided with their dislike of seeing German money cross the Alps. Thus he had political as well as religious backing, and was helped in addition by some of the scholars of the German Renaissance.

Though a university professor, Luther (1483-1546) was not a humanist. In thinking that all learning, save that which promised a truer understanding of the Bible, was irrelevant to Christianity he was mediæval where Erasmus was modern, and reminds us of the mystics who had thought that books were at best superfluous and at worst a stumbling-block. Intellectually conservative, even narrow, Luther never

[1] Froude, *Life and Letters of Erasmus*, p. 337.
[2] *Eng. Hist. Rev.*, Jan., 1920, p. 19.

freed his mind from the cloister he bodily fled. To him the Pope was Antichrist. He clung to a magical interpretation of the sacraments and was intolerant of other branches of the reform movement. He was anxious to save all that he could from the wreckage of the old faith. But his conservative mind was harnessed to a revolutionary temperament. An ex-monk, he married a nun. In his "Address to the Nobles," he appealed from ecclesiastical prejudice to secular fair-mindedness. He challenged the Papacy by nailing up his Theses, and defied it by burning its Bull: at Worms he outfaced the Empire. And all the while he knew what had happened to Hus, and gloried in the chance of martyrdom.[1]

This antagonism between intellect and character was reflected both in his own life and in the history of the Lutheran reformation. To Luther himself, troubled by a ceaseless conflict between faith and reason, reason savoured of devil's work. Among his followers, divisions soon arose from his inconsistency of teaching and conduct. He sought inspiration direct from the literal reading of the Bible instead of through the medium of tradition, but he never allowed complete freedom of scriptural interpretation as a universal right: he affirmed the priesthood and equality of every Christian, but he allowed his democratic ideal to bend and break before his innate reverence for princes. In depreciating the value of external religion, he underrated the necessity of the Church as an organization, and was driven to rely upon the princes instead. Luther's reformation was thus confused with the political ambitions of the princes, and the Divine Right of Popes was replaced by the Divine Right of Kings.

Luther's ultimate failure no less than his early success was part of his greatness. The failure of

[1] See his letter to his father (1521) where he says he wants to be burned or slaughtered by the Pope. *Martin Luther: Eine Auswahl aus seinen Schriften.* Ed. Neubauer, p. 149.

Erasmus, like that of many another, was the fault of circumstance. For Luther, towering above even the greatest figures of the Renaissance, success and failure alike were conditioned by his own personality. In any age, in any land, his force of character would have sufficed to uproot the deepest foundations of ancient usage, to compel people not only to examine and criticize the structure which, grumble as they might, they had always considered as part of their daily lives, but also to call in question the ideas that had caused its creation.

A single page chosen at random from Luther's shorter and simpler writings offers an unforgettable glimpse of the man's courage, of his conviction, and above all of his flawless sincerity. To his father he tells of his hot youth, his spiritual conflicts and his contempt for martyrdom with the same simplicity, almost in the same breath. Certain that the life of the spirit is maintained by the faith within a man and not otherwise, he neither feared nor reverenced outward things in themselves. He knew that the threats and persecutions of the Church could not touch his " inward, spiritual man," he knew that the Pope could not cut off a single soul from God by an interdict, but he believed fervently in the malign power of a personal Devil. This preoccupation with the " things of the spirit " did not make him inhuman, partly because his mind was essentially concrete.[1] Here he parted company with the mystics. Though for him the communion between God and man was an " inward " experience, he opposed the mystical conception of God as the timeless, unchanging Absolute, to whom good and evil, joy and sorrow are one. He said he did not want the visions and extasies of the mystic's life. His God was the Carpenter of Nazareth, who grew from a baby into a man, who suffered, made friends,

[1] For this and for much of the rest of this paragraph see T. R. Glover, *The Pilgrim*, pp. 179–189.

loved children and poor people, who gave his message to the world and died a criminal's death. Luther himself was fond of children and family life, jokes and music and chess, and, not least of all, the German tongue which he helped to fashion.

But in his view, the good of all outward things follows from spiritual blessedness. They are an effect, not a cause. Good works, hallowed clothes and sacred places, fasting and long prayers may be part of a hypocrite's daily life; therefore they have no power to make a man good. He could speak from experience. While he had lived the monastic life he later denounced, he permanently injured himself by his austerities, and gave himself the right to say that if anyone could have been saved by monkery it was Martin Luther. But good works, he says, come from a good man as naturally as good fruit from a good tree. They are the outward expression of an inward union with Christ. They cannot achieve that union, which comes only by possession of God's Word by Faith. For the soul of a believer will become what the Word is, " gleich als das Eisen wirt glutrot wie das Feur aus der Vereinigung mit dem Feur."[1] Faith alone, so far as a man is a spirit, suffices him for all freedom and holiness and goodness, but since he has a body, the outward work of discipline will be necessary to keep his body in obedience. Good works are also the link that binds the Christian to his fellow. They are the manifestation of love. " . . . ein Christenmensch lebt nit in ihm selb, sondern in Christo und seinem Nähsten: in Christo durch den Glauben, im Nähsten durch die Liebe."[2]

Inconsistency could not be avoided by a man whose spiritual existence was on the one hand independent of outward things, and on the other the mainspring of a vital personality which forced him to play a leading

---

[1] *Martin Luther: Eine Auswahl aus seinen Schriften.* Ed. Neubauer, p. 133.   [2] *Ib.*, p. 138.

part in the public affairs of his age, to believe in facts rather than theories, to rely upon experience instead of logic. There is no logical outward expression of spiritual convictions. What institution could embody Luther's fundamental paradox that " a Christian man is free and lord of all things, and is yet bound and the servant of all " ? How, in spite of his wish not to be revolutionary, could anything essential to the old Church remain if the priesthood of every Christian were recognized ? How could the equality of all men be reconciled with obedience to the powers that are ordained of God ? Luther's reformation went too far for the Catholics and not far enough for the Protestants; and it did not offer a half-way house. This is perhaps the surest proof of the man's power : he forced everybody to move. After he had re-stated the teaching of Christ, it was no longer possible to stand still, to be content with patching the old Church, or to leave religion as he left it. Orthodox and Protestant alike were compelled to build anew.

The inconsistent and inadequate Lutheran movement was naturally opposed not only by the increasing pressure of the old Church but by a series of new revivals of which the aim was to discover a simpler yet more secure position than that offered by Luther and his followers. The most important achievement of the other Protestant revolutions was the " Reformed Church " of Calvin (1509-1564). From its centre at Geneva, where Calvin's chair still stands in the cathedral, its teaching was widespread over Scotland, France, Holland and the South German towns.

A Frenchman, a lawyer, and a humanist, Calvin was more practical and more logical than Luther. His gifts were for organization, administration and the writing of prose rather than for constructive theology, for which we owe him next to nothing. The differences between the leaders reappeared in the differences between the two reformations. In their zeal to sacrifice everything not expressly sanctioned by the Scriptures the Calvinists were opposed to the Lutherans. The Lutherans worked through the princes, the Calvinists through the people. The Lutherans had no independent system of government; the Calvinists had a rigid theocracy. The Calvinists were deeply influenced by the Renaissance, which affected the Lutherans comparatively little, yet they were far more intolerant than the Lutherans.

Calvin's problem in Geneva was to found an organization by which an inward change of faith could be expressed in an outward way of life. His solution was the theocratic polity which the Genevese accepted at his hands. He allowed of no division between Church and State: the Church was the State. Ministers of the Church were officers of state. Each minister had to undergo careful training before his final election by the citizens; if his conduct were scandalous he might be reduced to the rank of an ordinary citizen. The chief court of the State, a consistory of ministers and elders, was also elected. It was the guardian of the people's morals and had civil as well as spiritual functions. From its sentences there was no appeal.

This fusion of a religious ideal with a practical form of government made Calvinism spread more rapidly than Lutheranism had done, but the attempt to clothe religion in the strait-waistcoat of an institution has always had disastrous effects. In the Calvinistic theocracy, for instance, heresy was clearly treason, since to deny the Church was to deny the State, and the Calvinists did not shrink from the bitter intolerance to which they were pledged by the recognition of this fact. Intolerance, however, was a characteristic common to nearly all sects of the second generation of reformers. Less tolerant than the early Lutherans, they were far less tolerant than the mediæval Church.

The achievements of the Reformation in constructive theological thought do not seem to have been great: most of the leaders' teaching could be found in the writings either of the Fathers or else in those of the mediæval scholastics. But the critical spirit which produced that teaching was a startling achievement because it was a guarantee of ultimate liberty to individual minds. Its immediate result of a number of new communions was an immense gain. Their further subdivision was the pledge of their mutual tolerance, for the smaller the divisions, the less the coercive power at the disposal of each. So in time a *modus vivendi* was certain to be found.

A second immediate achievement of the Reformation was an increased purity and sincerity in religion. In the Middle Ages to die for a belief had been accounted madness: none the worse had been thought of the many heretics who recanted. But the Reformation gave such reality to the inward conviction of religious truth that in parting with his faith a man thought to lose his soul.

One of the greatest triumphs of the Reformation was the reform of the old Church. What the reformers failed to do within the Church, they effected by their despairing resolution to leave it: by creating a Reformation without, they induced a Counter-Reformation within. The Counter-Reformation was not, however, merely a reaction. It was, in one sense, the culmination of the urgent efforts to cleanse the Church made all through the fifteenth and sixteenth centuries by men who remained true to the orthodox faith. Of these efforts the most interesting, because the most liberal, was the work of the " middle party " led by Contarini and Giberti. These men were not only anxious to set on foot a drastic reform of ecclesiastical discipline and organization, but were willing to make considerable sacrifices of dogma. In 1541 they met the Lutherans at Ratisbon, and both parties succeeded in arriving at an agreement on the doctrines of original sin, free will and justification. The moderate Catholics would have permitted even the marriage of priests and the administration of the communion in both kinds to laymen. But Contarini, to whom " all true dominion was the dominion of reason," failed to make his views prevail. The two groups of reformers could not agree on the subject of the sacraments nor on that of the papal prerogative; there was already a divergence of opinion in the Catholic group; Luther was mistrustful, and the King of France was doing his best to foster religious discord between the Emperor and the Protestants. All hopes of avoiding the desperate struggles between the old and new faiths were thus dissolved: the narrower, less liberal Catholic revival, known as the Counter-Reformation, never attempted anything more constructive than annihilation of the Reformed churches and the consolidation and strict definition of Roman Catholic organization and dogma.

Before the Colloquy of Ratisbon, a strong Catholic revival was taking place in Spain. This owed nothing to the Papacy, which was kept at a respectful distance by the Spanish sovereigns: it was a purely national movement led by Spanish bishops and religious leaders. Even the Spanish Inquisition was under royal, not papal, control. Spanish religion, like Spanish gold, overflowed the borders of Spain. As Spanish imperialism was crowned by the ideal of Catholic unity, as Spanish armaments led the van of the old faith in the Religious Wars, so Spanish bishops gave direction and honesty and learning to the Council of Trent, and so the Spanish Loyola (1491-1556) sent forth the members of his Company to spread the seed of the purified faith over all the kingdoms of the world.

The policy and character of the Counter-Reformation was decided by the Council of Trent which lasted for nearly twenty years (1545-1563). In spite of the selfishness of the Popes and of the numerous Italian representatives, in spite of the refusal of the Protestants to attend its meetings, in spite of the narrowness imparted to its decisions by hostility to the reformed churches, the Council, thanks chiefly to its Spanish members, did lasting work for the old Church. The reform and purification of the monastic orders was taken in hand, and provision was made for the better education of the clergy. The result, as Erasmus could have foretold, was an improvement in the manners of the clergy, in the general level of religious sincerity, and above all in a general increase of respect for the Roman Church. The unity of the Church, and hence its fighting strength, was ensured by doctrinal decisions which disarmed moderate reformers and heretics alike. Sacramental questions and the problems of justification by faith, free will and clerical marriage were settled in the mediæval sense. It was definitely laid down at Trent that the use and custom of the Church had the validity of law, and that the Vulgate[1] was the only authentic version of the Scriptures. This restored to the Pope his mediæval supremacy. In addition, it was decided that the authority of the Pope was superior to that of a General Council, and that the Pope had the sole right of interpreting ecclesiastical writings, including the decrees made at Trent. Thus, in the chief matters of dispute between the old and new faiths, compromise was ruled out.

Its policy decided, the Counter-Reformation was carried on by several kinds of machinery. First there was the remodelled Papacy. On the ecclesiastical side the Papacy had lost its comprehensive dominion. The uncompromising decisions of the Council not only completed the severance of the Protestants from Rome, but to some extent lessened papal influence over Catholic states. Not a single government outside Portugal, Italy and Poland consented

[1] As revised by the Council.

to swallow whole the Tridentine decrees. But on the political side, the Papacy, by defining and consolidating its power in a smaller sphere, probably gained much more than it lost. It became a workable modern state instead of an obsolete universal government. As head of the Roman Inquisition the Pope condemned and executed the heretic, thus uniting the prerogatives of Church and State. If he could no longer influence imperial destinies by resting a peaceful finger on the map of the world, he could take a respectable part in the concourse of the new monarchies. Unlike the Holy Roman Emperor, he had solved the political problem of the Renaissance.

Next there were the Index and the Inquisition. These gave to the Catholic Church in fullness of power what it had lost in comprehensiveness of appeal. They were to guard the purity of Church teaching; to control the minds of the laity. The Tridentine Index was published in 1564. Books were examined, modified or condemned if necessary, and catalogues issued of forbidden literature. As usual Spain was more thorough than Rome: and the " Index Expurgatorius " was a Spanish and not a Roman institution.[1]

The Inquisition was originally a mediæval institution used for the suppression of the Albigenses in Southern France and was only under the partial control of the Papacy. It had been revived in Spain by Ferdinand and Isabella to coerce the Jews. On the advice of Spaniards, a body modelled on this Spanish Inquisition was set up in Rome by the Pope in 1542. It had greater powers than the mediæval inquisition had possessed, and it was brought more definitely under papal control. Its operations were confined to Italy: in the Netherlands it was Spain and not the Pope who tried to introduce inquisitorial machinery. There can be no doubt of the immediate success of the Inquisition. Both in Spain and Italy

[1] Acton: *Lectures on Modern History*, pp. 120–121.

the blood of the martyrs drowned the seed of their Church. After the sixteenth century the Inquisition was used less and less. It had done its work.

Thirdly the Counter-Reformation worked through the new religious Orders which had sprung up in Spain and Italy in answer to the general outcry against the old monks and friars. The Franciscan Order was born again in the Order of the Capuchins, which still survives. The Theatines tried to combine the Franciscan ideals of poverty, preaching and care of the sick with the ecclesiastical duties of secular clergy. But the Society of Jesus (1539), most important of all the new Orders, succeeded best in keeping the strength and discarding the weakness of the old systems. The Jesuits kept the three strict vows of monasticism. They kept the Franciscan ideal of working in the world, but practised it in a new way. They became men of the world in order to influence the powerful, and for the same reason they worked among the rich rather than among the poor. They discarded monkish attire with monkish ideals of asceticism; they gave up the monastic tradition of innumerable services and prayers. In their government they kept the policy of the old Regular Orders in maintaining independence of the bishops and direct dependence on the Papacy. But their government was much more efficient and more highly organized than that of the older Orders,—indeed, considered as a piece of machinery, it probably worked more smoothly than any government invented before or since. The secret of its success lay in its power of suppressing individuality: the Jesuits came nearer than anyone outside Plato's Republic to merging the individual in his community. The only democratic element in the constitution was the election of the General. Once elected he had almost uncontrolled power. He had, it is true, to listen to a consultative council imposed on him by the General Congregation. But he was not obliged to act upon its advice, and he could dispense individuals from its decrees although it was the highest legislative body in the Order. Yet even the General was not to be allowed to clog the machine. Under definite circumstances he could be deposed.

The Jesuits owed much of their success to their educational system. Though their views were conservative, even retrogressive, their methods were modern. They avoided both the early Franciscan distrust of learning and the intellectual conservatism of the later friars and monks. Like Erasmus, they appreciated what was best in the old thought and in the new. They accepted the theology of Aquinas, but they made use of Renaissance scholarship and educational methods. They went far beyond monastic achievements as educators of boys, and imposed so long and thorough an educational training on their own members that those who entered the highest grade of the Order looked back upon some thirty years of preparation.

The difference between the old Orders and the Jesuits was fundamental. To the old Orders a life lived in obedience to their Rule was an end in itself, since it was a service to God; to the Jesuits their strictly regulated life was but an instrument to an end. And instruments must be kept sharp and efficient. The end the Jesuits had in view was to win back Europe to the old faith. Their work embraced the whole vast religious problem of the day. They sought not only to remedy the causes of the Reformation, but to reverse the Reformation itself. They raised a new army of clerics who went far by their lives to take away the reproach of the pre-Reformation clergy. They took charge of Catholic dogma, defending it, explaining it, and attacking its enemies in able pamphlets. They became the political agents of the Counter-Reformation in every country of Europe. As confessors of Catholic kings they could use their advantage to press the interests of the Counter-Reformation, as spies in Protestant countries they could incite to assassination and collect useful information; anywhere and at any time, with all the persuasiveness and logic at their command, they would press some doctrine to justify the end they had in view at the moment. Thus at one stage they were advocating notions of extreme democracy and tyrannicide, while at another they were the mainstay of absolutism. In addition, they were the emissaries of the Counter-Reformation to heretics and heathen. They won back much of Germany and the whole of Poland to the old faith. They only just failed to win back Sweden. They planted and governed Paraguay and helped to explore Canada in the Far West; they busied themselves in the Far East, " walking by missions through the dry places of China, Japan and the Indies."[1] Above all, they were the teachers of the Counter-Reformation, and set themselves to win the future for their faith. In their schools and colleges a sound classical education was given free on strict religious lines. These institutions were, for a long while, numerous and efficient, and were the chief means of secondary education in Europe until well on in the eighteenth century. " As for the pedagogical part," said Bacon, " the shortest rule would be, consult the schools of the Jesuits; for nothing better has been put in practice." Most of the eighteenth-century French philosophers who were so bitterly hostile to the Jesuits owed their education to Jesuit foundations.

The last weapon of the Counter-Reformation leaders was the secular power of Catholic kings and magnates. But the Reformers matched them there, boasting the support of rival crowns. This political weapon was, in addition, one over which neither side had much control. Even Philip II had political as well as religious aims, and the most important results of the Thirty Years War were, not the religious partition

[1] Hobbes, *Leviathan* (Everyman's Lib.), p. 383.

of Germany, but the consolidation of French and Swedish power and the sanction of German particularism. Whichever faith the kings adopted they intended to gain more from religion than they gave it, till it became clear enough that the liberty claimed for individuals or churches by the religious leaders of the sixteenth century would never be achieved under the government of those whose dearest wish was to imitate the despotism of Louis XIV.

CHAPTER III

LEVIATHAN

"Celui, qui a donné des rois au monde a voulu qu'ils fussent honorés commes ses représantants en se reservant à lui seul le droit de juger de ses actions. Celui qui est né sujet doit obéir sans murmurer ; telle est sa volonté."
Louis XIV (Bluntschli, *Theory of the State*, p. 288).

". . . If he transferre the Militia, he retains the Judicature in vain, for want of execution of the Lawes : Or if he grant away the Power of raising Mony ; the Militia is in vain : or if he give away the government of Doctrines, men will be frighted into rebellion with the feare of Spirits."
Hobbes, *Leviathan*, c. 18 (Everyman's Lib. Ed.).

". . . Or that we in England should not with the last drop of blood defend this almost only spot of ground which seems remaining in the world to publick Liberty."
Sir Charles Davenant, 1695, *Ways and Means of Supplying the War* (works, Vol. I, p. 5, London, 1771).

THE triumph of the Renaissance state is the most obvious fact of seventeenth-century history. Built originally on the feudal land-holding monarchies, each Renaissance kingdom was still in the seventeenth century in a sense the property of its ruler. Even in the following century it seemed proper for states to be inherited, while uninherited kingship savoured of usurpation.[1] It was still natural in the eighteenth century that states should be transferred by will or by marriage from one ruler to another. They could even be partitioned or sold without a

[1] In Russia Peter the Great had provided that every Tsar should choose his own successor but in 1797 Catherine's son Paul reintroduced primogeniture. *Camb. Mod. Hist.*, VI, 681.

thought for the wishes of the inhabitants. State boundaries were limited merely by the competitive strength of monarchs : nationality as a right and privilege of citizens did not exist.

In the same way religion as a right of citizens did not exist. The Reformation, instead of achieving at once the liberty of the individual, only achieved in the first instance the liberty of rulers. Luther, by appealing to the princes, made them ecclesiastical arbiters. "Cujus regio ejus religio" meant that kings had the divine right to choose their religion; the people could merely choose their ruler by moving from one state to another. Henry VIII, though he wrote a treatise against Luther, followed the Lutheran idea in making himself supreme head of the Church in England. Speaking roughly, the religion of the English people changed with each change in the ecclesiastical policy of the government. Calvin went the other way to work and made the religious head the chief civil magistrate. But as far as liberty was concerned the result was always the same—the individual had no freedom in religious matters.

As a matter of fact, just because Calvinists and Presbyterians did establish a religious tyranny which was in its essence a challenge to the secular state, they materially served the cause of liberty in spite of themselves. In England, Holland and France they vigorously asserted the rights of a minority against the overriding claims of the Renaissance state.[1] Hobbes definitely accused the Presbyterians of this.[2]

The Lutherans, on the contrary, although Luther himself championed the claims of the individual conscience, increased the power of the state against the liberty of individuals or of groups.

For Luther, Christendom was still one, but he exalted the secular power and abased the power of the Church.

[1] Figgis, *From Gerson to Grotius*, p. 75.
[2] *Leviathan*, 377.

The Kingdom of God was invisible and spiritual, but orthodox Catholics and Protestant Anabaptists alike were guilty of confusing this unearthly City of God with an earthly Church armed with material power. Yet God had provided the visible state as the true repository of power on earth. Therefore ecclesiastical power is usurped, but the power of the state is good and given by God. All earthly jurisdiction and coercion belongs by divine right to the state, to the state all other organizations are subject, from the state all law is derived. Resistance to the state is therefore resistance to God.

This theory might have served the Emperor, for whom Luther had great reverence; it might have served a feudal oligarchy or even a democratic assembly. But because the princes had the chief power in Germany Luther was driven by his practical sense to rely on them. This is why Lutheranism served the cause of Renaissance monarchy.

Luther's contribution to despotism was the religious and moral sanction that he gave to Machiavelli's utilitarian notions of an omnicompetent ruler, of an obedient people, of a unified state. In France, some supporters of Henry IV added a legal sanction by asserting the hereditary nature of sovereignty by divine right, a doctrine which was developed later from a different standpoint by the Anglican supporters of the Stuart régime. Kingship by hereditary divine right was the apotheosis of monarchy. Against it there could be no appeal. Unlike the utilitarian sovereignties of Machiavelli and Hobbes, its title was not damaged by inefficiency. Again, whereas Machiavelli and Hobbes were willing to entertain the notion of a sovereign assembly provided its government were efficient, kingship by hereditary divine right could be vested only in a single person.

In the middle of the seventeenth century, this political dream came true in the government of France.

We noticed earlier the general political and economic foundations of the new monarchy. Its final realization in France was due to Henry IV and Richelieu.

At the opening of Henry IV's reign, France was exhausted by the religious wars and distracted by their aftermath of anarchy. The nobility had reaped the full advantage from the unsettlement of the times, and the Edict of Nantes confirmed to the Huguenots, in addition to their religious liberty, certain political privileges which, by making them almost autonomous, threatened the unity of the state. Their political ideal was a federation of small and virtually independent communes—an ideal which was the direct antithesis of the close-knit Renaissance state, but which was revived in after years by the Girondists.

By respecting not only the religious liberty of the Huguenots but also the political anomaly of their independent towns, Henry reduced suspicion and unrest. He bridled the ambitions of the nobility by harshness after conspiracy, by the prohibition of duelling, and by the institution of the *paulette*. This last was a tax on payment of which an office-holder might transmit his office to his heir. It therefore helped to create an hereditary aristocracy of civil service as opposed to the hereditary caste of birth and military distinction. Something was done for the prosperity of the country by the encouragement of industry but more especially of agriculture, and also by the close supervision of the financial system which was so bad that the government was said to receive only one-quarter of the taxes which the people paid.

It may be said that in merely patching the existing institutions of France, Henry was laying up trouble for his successors. The financial system, depending on the principle of farming out the taxes to subordinates, was thoroughly bad and ought to have been reconstructed. An hereditary civil service increased the number of privileged classes that were to prove a curse to the country. And the political privileges in the Edict of Nantes (1598) paved the way for rebellion on the one side, for persecution on the other. All this is true. But like Elizabeth in England, Henry understood that his reign was a time for caution. Just as he refrained from a militant foreign policy, so at home he refrained from radical innovations. He was justified by the event, for the measure of security and prosperity he gave to France greatly strengthened the position of the crown and went far to consolidate the state.

Within France, as abroad, much of his work was undone after his death by his widow, only to be restored and developed later by Richelieu (1585-1642). Richelieu's one object was the supremacy of the crown. His passion was for France, not for the dynasty, but he considered that the greatness of his country depended upon the strength of the king. Richelieu had to overcome the hostility of the court,—no easy matter,—before he could put his policy to the test, and as long as there was no direct heir to the throne his hands were partly tied by the conspiracies of members of the royal family. The ultimate birth of an heir (1638), the future Louis XIV, put the highest prize of rebellion out of contention's reach, and justified the Cardinal for having passed from the defence of the crown to its aggrandisement.

He had already caused the aristocracy to find rebellion a two-edged weapon, for insurrection was made by him an excuse for extreme severity. Many of the greatest lords paid for their temerity with their heads; those who escaped with their lives had to live them in a narrowed sphere. By destroying their castles Richelieu enforced the lesson he was determined to teach them, the lesson that they, like other people, were subject to the law; and by transferring their chief functions as provincial governors to the Intendants, paid servants of the crown but hitherto of comparatively little importance, he broke the administrative and political power of the nobility and deprived it of some of its wealth.

If Richelieu regarded the nobles as enemies, he wanted the clerics of all creeds for friends. He opposed extremists of all kinds, whether Jesuit, Jansenist or Huguenot, because he knew that fanaticism is never amenable to reasons of state. His ecclesiastical ideal, for the sake of political unity, was religious reunion, but, aiming only at what was possible, he was always ready to give high office to able Huguenots, and to safeguard their freedom of worship. What he refused to stomach was their political power, which clearly threatened the unity of the kingdom. Richelieu besieged the chief Huguenot town of La Rochelle, and on its fall deprived the Protestants of their political privileges, which they never recovered.

Richelieu's Intendants did not only replace the nobility to some extent; they also took over many of the powers and privileges of the provincial assemblies. The central assembly, the States General, he never summoned. As a matter of fact, owing to its lack of financial and legislative control, the States General had ceased to be of importance since the close of the fifteenth century, and was never summoned after 1614 until the eve of the Revolution.

Whether Richelieu's policy was beneficial to France in the long run may be disputed. It is clear, for instance, that his autocratic methods of administration, including his perversion of justice and his control of the press, were preparing the way for revolution. He failed unquestionably in the economic sphere. He created the French navy, but he neglected agriculture and manufactures. His ideal of political unity does not seem to have embraced economic unity; he did not remove the provincial tolls and customs duties which were a serious hindrance to trade Above all, he did nothing to improve the finances. But from Richelieu's own political point of view, his life-work was an unqualified success. Abroad he had defeated the Hapsburgs: at home he had made of France a unified autocratic state.

When Louis XIV came to power, the only possible source of constitutional resistance was the Parlement of Paris, the most important court of justice in France. The Parlement was more than a powerful corporate body. It possessed the right to register the king's edicts before they were executed. If it refused to register an edict, the king could override its decision only by a special process, which might perhaps be compared with the English king's power of creating peers. Thus the Parlement possessed an imperfect and indirect veto on legislation. Richelieu had snubbed this ancient body, but at the time of the Great Rebellion in England, when Louis XIV was a child and when Mazarin, the chief minister in France, was much hated, the Parlement led a constitutional movement for financial and administrative reform. If it had been successful, Louis might have become a limited monarch instead of an autocrat. But the constitutional movement was entangled with the Fronde (1648-1652), that last factious uprising of the French nobility which was successfully defeated by Mazarin. The Cardinal died soon afterwards (1661). From that time onwards the king was supreme, and he refused ever to have another prime minister. Like Philip II in Spain, Louis governed by means of councils, and like Philip he deprived the provincial assemblies of their powers, though he still tolerated their existence.

Louis's despotism was religious no less than political, at least in aim. At the beginning of his reign his control over the Church was not complete. The Jesuits were his staunch allies, but the Papacy and the Gallican Church had certain independent rights in Church government: the Huguenots and Jansenists were rebels in matters of faith.

For unity of faith he paid a high price. The

Huguenots had shown by peacefulness that they deserved their toleration. They had taken no part in the Fronde. Louis hoped at first that they would re-enter the national church by consent. When they refused, he tried to convert them, first by giving rewards for their apostasy, and later by persecuting their constancy. Finally he betrayed his own honour in 1685 by revoking the Edict of Nantes which he had promised faithfully to observe. Calvinism was driven underground by persecution, or forced to seek a remedy in illegal emigration, which enriched the neighbours of France as much as it impoverished herself.

Then there were the Jansenists. Their sect had arisen in Richelieu's time and had attracted a large and influential following. They were Catholics with Puritan leanings: they believed in the universal Church and in the authority of tradition, but they held Calvinistic views on predestination. Whether their teachings were heretical or not long remained a matter for discussion. But there was no doubt about their hostility to the Jesuits, whose intellectual ascendancy they undermined fatally by the brilliant satire of Pascal's *Provincial Letters* (1656). The Pope condemned them, though at one stage they were in the strange position of supporting the Papacy against the king and the Jesuits. For many years they lived under the cloud of royal and orthodox displeasure, and at the close of his reign Louis persecuted them not less cruelly, though with less permanent success, than he had persecuted the Huguenots.

It proved easier to secure unity of worship than to bring the Church completely under royal control. If the Gallican Church had stood alone, matters might have been comparatively simple. The French bishops were more afraid of papal encroachments than of royal interference: they needed the king's protection against the Pope. In spite of this Louis failed to free himself of papal control.

Some of the king's ministers and many of his most eminent lawyers wished him to follow Henry VIII—to sever the connection between France and Rome, and to make himself supreme head of the Gallican Church. Both in France and at Rome there was talk of a possible schism. But the bishops themselves did not bear the thought of it with equanimity. More important still, both Louis and the Pope were afraid of it: they were too useful to each other. The Pope condemned the Jansenists at Louis's request and turned a blind eye to the irregularities of his private life. Innocent XI on his side always hoped that Louis would renounce his friendship with the Sultan and lead a crusade against the Turks.

Consequently, although for nearly thirty years of the reign Louis and the Pope were disputing over one thing or another, sometimes with the greatest bitterness, Innocent never acted violently except when he excommunicated Louis's ambassador, and Louis himself always stopped short of a final breach. However haughty an attitude he might adopt, it was always he and not the Pope who made concessions in their quarrels: when Louis hoped to secure his reward for revoking the Edict of Nantes, all the ungrateful Innocent did was to ask what the use might be of destroying heretical places of worship in a country where the bishops themselves were on the verge of schism. By 1692 Innocent XI was dead, but the papal victory was secure.

No doubt Louis's failure was due partly to his own blunders, partly to the complications of his foreign policy, but it was due still more to the incompatibility of his aims. The plain fact is that a Catholic king could not be the "compleat" Renaissance despot. If he insisted on loyalty to a Church with an international government he could not expect to bring it under the control of a national despotism. Even the Venetian oligarchy, which excluded clerics from governmental posts and claimed complete independence of Rome save in purely doctrinal matters, abated some of its claims when Henry IV mediated between Venice and the Pope. It is a clear proof of Louis's power that in France, where tradition favoured a much closer connection with Rome, the issue was so long in suspense.

Louis wanted to be absolute in learning and literature no less than in politics and religion. Richelieu had founded the French academy and the first French newspaper. Louis founded and patronized other intellectual institutions and liked to keep men of letters about him. But he did not favour either learning or literature for their own sakes; he valued them merely as aids to the completion of his autocracy. Free expression was made impossible by his strict censorship. Control of the press was part of the usual stock-in-trade of Renaissance monarchy. Before religious controversy became acute, the freedom of the infant press was not seriously disturbed, but the Reformation helped to stifle intellectual no less than political individuality. The Popes were not the only censors. In almost every state, whether Protestant or not, king and clergy could and did condemn books, order them to be burnt, and punish not only their authors but their printers and publishers. Hobbes insisted on the need of uniformity of doctrine for security of state : otherwise " men will be frighted into rebellion with the feare of Spirits."[1] We shall see in the next chapter how the French literature of the period often lent itself to the king's glory, but how on the other hand French thought was sometimes forced to seek expression outside France.

In nothing was Louis XIV more successful than in his social despotism, which was European in its sway. Here as elsewhere most of the spade-work had been done for him : by the time he ascended the throne French civilization was second to none. We know

[1] *Leviathan*, c. 18.

what Evelyn thought of seventeenth century Paris. "And truly Paris," he writes in 1643, ". . . is one of the most gallant cities in the world," and then he compares it with London:—" there is no comparison between the buildings, palaces and materials, these being entirely of stone and more sumptuous, though I esteem our piazzas to exceed theirs."[1] His most glowing descriptions are kept for the gardens, of which he seems to have liked best the one belonging to the Luxembourg Palace. " What is most admirable, you see no gardeners or men at work, and yet all is kept in such exquisite order, as if they did nothing else but work ; it is so early in the morning, that all is dispatched and done without the least confusion."[2] This could stand for a description of Paris to-day. Yet Louis was not content with Paris, which, after all, in spite of its regality had always been the storm-centre of disaffection and not the haven of monarchy. It was outside Paris that he raised a fit dwelling for his pride. With a perverse lavishness that seems to have come straight out of the *Arabian Nights* he chose a wilderness for his site. At the word of a king and at the cost of millions, fountains sprang from the arid soil, and elaborate gardens, full of rare plants and trees, overspread the desert, while French wealth took visible form in the vast magnificence of the Versailles palace. Still an arresting witness to the force and splendour of Renaissance despotism, Versailles was made by Louis the social centre not only of France but of Europe. It was there that he patronized the great writers who lent their lustre to his reign ; there that the rigid etiquette was evolved, the splendid fashions displayed, and the brilliant language perfected that made the social fiat of Versailles obeyed all over civilized Europe. It was there, too, that Louis gave the *coup de grâce* to the feudal aristocracy. In the brilliant society of Versailles

[1] *Evelyn's Diary*, ed. Wm. Bray, 1854, Vol. I, pp. 45, 65.
[2] *Ib.*, p. 64.

the nobility at last found a constant lure which finally singed them with penury and incompetence, but whose attractions they were unable to resist. Many a proud office of state owes its origin to some personal service rendered to a lord in days when government was an extension of the private life of an individual. In the seventeenth century, when government was safely divorced from court life, Louis revived the old intimate ties and duties that were never again to be allied to political power. The French *noblesse* were encouraged to spend their time and money in the gilded society of Versailles while their contemporaries across the channel were shouldering the burdens of Parliamentary business and rural administration.

Political absolutism was paralleled by Louis' mercantilist economic policy. To a seventeenth century government, the mercantile system was one of the numerous instruments of the Renaissance state. Like the state churches, state commerce had political ends. The great economic problem for rulers was how to make trade and commerce increase the power of the state. That power must be increased in three ways. First, to meet the heavy expenses of the Renaissance monarchies with their diplomatic and civil services, their armies and their judicial systems, the revenues of the crown must be increased. Secondly, considering that war was the rule and peace the exception, plenty of gold must be kept in the state. This gold reserve served the purpose of the modern national debt. Thirdly, the state must be self-supporting in order to survive in its hostile surroundings. Ministers and merchants,—who did not always agree,—showed the kings how these needs might be satisfied. Several ways of increasing royal revenues were tried in the seventeenth century, among them being improved methods of taxation and royal intervention in trade by the grant of monopolies and patents or by the king's turning merchant himself.

If kings wanted to keep gold in their dominions chiefly because of its great use in wars, merchants wanted a good supply of it because people of all countries would accept it in exchange for their own produce. By the seventeenth century general opinion was agreed that legislation was useless to prevent the export of gold. The gain of smuggling a commodity of which small quantities were so valuable was out of all proportion to the risk involved. But the "mercantilists" argued that if home manufacturers and merchants were encouraged to make commodities and export them, and if foreigners were discouraged from sending in their goods, then the exports of a country would exceed its imports, and the amount of this excess would be received in gold and silver, "those bewitching and domineering mettals."[1] All that the government had to do to keep gold in the country was to encourage exports and to discourage imports. But as there was no international credit system, merchants trading with tropical countries wanted to take gold out of their own country to pay for tropical goods whose owners would not part with them in exchange for the products of cold lands. So, later in the century, Dutch and English merchants took the trouble to show that even the export of gold brought in more gold. For the goods bought afar with Dutch or English gold could be sold again in Europe for more gold than had been used for buying them in the East.

Again, to make a country self-supporting, the government must encourage home manufacturers and discourage the foreigner. But it must not encourage the export of agricultural produce, of which, even if a surplus were produced, the whole must be retained as a precaution against high prices and famine in time of war.

This policy of fostering manufacture meant a demand

[1] Fabian Phillips, *Praeemption and Pourveyance*, 1663.

for colonies and ships—colonies for private markets and private stores of raw material, ships for carrying goods to markets and for bringing the raw material home. Further, it meant the imposition of high import duties and the reduction of export duties so as to discourage the foreigner and help the home manufacturer. Above all, it meant careful regulation and control. As the only body that could exercise effective control in the sixteenth and seventeenth centuries was the government, mercantilism was a policy of governmental interference in all departments of industry, trade and commerce.

This economic policy which reckoned wealth in terms of power and efficiency was adopted and put into effect with greater or less completeness by all the important states, whether they were despotic or not, of seventeenth and eighteenth century Europe. But France was the model, and Colbert, who hated holidays and clerics alike because they did not produce anything, was its most logical exponent.

Henry IV had encouraged French manufactures and the beginnings of French colonization in Canada, while his minister Sully had improved the working of the French financial system. But it was Colbert (1619-1683), the finance minister of Louis XIV, who made France the first of mercantile states. As steward of Mazarin's wealth, Colbert had had a useful financial training, for the Cardinal wanted all the luxuries wealth could buy, and at the same time to increase his fortune. Colbert enabled his master both to have his cake and eat it; and before Louis had started his expensive wars it seemed as if this faithful steward would do as much for the fortunes of France as he had already done for those of the Cardinal. The improvements he made in the financial administration had two main results: first, he made the distribution of the taxes less unjust than it had ever been before, and secondly, he made the revenue received by the government approximate for the first time in the history of France to the amount of taxes imposed. To stimulate manufacture he abolished most of the local customs and tolls, and greatly improved both the water and road transport of the country. His celebrated Languedoc Canal was the "envy and despair" of other nations. He encouraged production, too, by imposing heavy import duties and removing export duties. But he favoured producers only because and if he thought they increased the wealth, that is the power, of the state. He prohibited the export of corn in the interests of the state. This discouraged farmers because France was at the time one of the chief corn producers of Europe. But Colbert dreaded high prices and scarcity in times of war. In the commercial sphere Colbert was especially successful. In particular, his ordinance of 1681 became the common maritime law of Europe, and in general his achievements were so great as to alarm foreign statesmen: it was believed in England, for instance, that he might make France the chief market of the world.[1]

With all its faults in theory and practice it seems that a mercantilist policy was on the whole the right one for seventeenth century statesmen to adopt. Wars were frequent; nations were in their industrial infancy; the highly developed international credit system of to-day did not exist. Even now there is something to be said for the protection of infant industries, and much to be said in the stress and aftermath of wars, when food is scarce and credit shaken, for government intervention to regulate the supply and distribution of food and to conserve the supply of gold.

But in the long run a mercantilist policy seems unwise. Its very success brings failure. For success is ever the best missionary, and mercantilism finds imitation too costly a flattery because its weapons can be turned against itself. High tariffs invite

[1] Hewins, *English Trade and Finance*, p. 133.

higher ones until the wall on either side is undermined by smuggling. Exclusiveness cannot be maintained without claim to the right of search: the enforcement of this claim engenders war. If war proved Colbert's justification it was also the ruin of his policy. Mercantilism might almost be called the parent, the child and the victim of war.

At the time of the Restoration in England, the great model state of France, infinitely nearer in achievement to its ideal than any work of mediæval times, seemed likely to absorb the whole of Europe, either by force of conquest or of attraction. The military power of France was immense: she threatened to draw Spain and England into her orbit, to engulf the Netherlands and part of Germany. Sweden had shared with France the spoils of Westphalia (1648), but these gains were the coping-stone of Swedish power, and merely the foundation of French supremacy. Everywhere the attraction of France was also at work. In England and in Germany she enslaved the courts to her political ideal; while all over Europe, but especially in Germany, her economic system, her language, her literature, her manners and her fashions in dress held sole and unquestioned sway in cultivated circles. By the close of the century even Holland had started to adopt French fashions, and rich Dutch families began to talk in French.

But the political contrast between France and Holland can scarcely be exaggerated. The constitution of Holland was more like that of the late German Empire than like that of any seventeenth century state. It was a group of seven different provinces with different institutions and interests, combining for certain purposes in a common federal government. One of these provinces, Holland, overtopped the other states in wealth, population and influence in the same way as Prussia dominated the other German states.

The chief officer of Holland, the Grand Pensionary, held much the same position of importance in the deliberations of the federal government as the Chancellor held in the imperial government of Germany. But Holland was weak where Prussia was strong. In Germany the ruling house which symbolized the unity of the empire was the ruling house of Prussia. In the United Provinces Holland was generally the enemy of the House of Orange. The House of Orange made its reputation by war: Holland made its wealth by peace. Holland was republican: the House of Orange monarchist. The republicans found their support among the trading population of the towns: the monarchists drew theirs from the agricultural population of the country. Consequently all through the greatest period of their history, the United Provinces were wavering between two political extremes: in times of peace and safety they were republican; in times of war they turned to monarchy.

But they never submitted to Renaissance sovereignty. The Dutch republic, whose towns and provinces possessed inherent and inalienable rights, was, like Switzerland, a survival of the mediæval "communitas communitatum." The Dutch writer, Althusius, founded his political theory on this fact, for he held that the state is a fellowship of groups, united for convenience by a central organ, but not deriving their existence and rights from it. In other words, by taking his stand on the polity of the United Provinces he could almost touch the mediæval world in the past and the United States of America in the future, surrounded though he was by the vast bulk of Leviathan.

What made the Dutch so much more important than the Swiss in this world of sovereign states was not, however, political theory but success. Because they attained greatness in spite of what public opinion could not but hold political weakness, they challenged

LEVIATHAN

the governmental tradition of the Renaissance, while at the same time they gave a new lease of life to the early spirit of enterprise and genius that had flowered in so many fields of fifteenth and sixteenth century life.

During the last part of her intermittent warfare with Spain, Holland burst without pause into her golden age which was as splendid as it was brief. It seemed as if the Dutch of this time had borrowed the words of an English contemporary to say to one another

> ". . . though we cannot make our sun
> Stand still, yet we will make him run."

In less than a century they produced painters who will never die—Rembrandt, Cuyp and Franz Hals; scientists and mathematicians whose lives were landmarks in the progress of human knowledge; writers who created a national language and founded new schools of thought; statesmen like John de Witt and William III who altered the course of history. Some of these acted many parts. Grotius (1583-1645) " excelled in almost every branch of knowledge and made himself a master of whatever subject he took in hand "[1]; John de Witt's political career might easily have been mathematical instead; and the elder Huyghens was statesman, diplomat, musician, linguist, poet and patron of art and letters. His son, Christian Huyghens, one of the ablest mathematicians the world has known, was also a brilliant inventor.

These were only a few of the most gifted men in a time when Holland was no less famous for art and science than for classical scholarship, music and theology—for the beauty of her books and the perfection of her maps. John Evelyn tells of his visit to the " famous printer Elzevir's printing-house and shop, renowned for the politeness of the character and

[1] Edmundson, *History of Holland*, p. 189.

editions of what he has published through Europe."[1] This was at Leyden, but the books produced by two publishers of Amsterdam were equally fine. At Leyden, William the Silent had founded a university, and less than two generations after his death, five other universities witnessed to the intellectual vitality of his country. Beyond academic circles, the rich and cultivated women of Holland shared in the Renaissance and helped to spread its influence. Some were as learned as any of their better-known forerunners in England and Italy; others, like the more famous French women of their own age and after, made learning fashionable in their salons, though one imagines that it must have needed more solid mental gifts to shine in the brilliant society of seventeenth century Amsterdam than in that of Paris a hundred years later.

This creative energy was not, as in France, fenced with orthodoxy and intolerance, but was allowed to expand as it listed in freedom of thought, speech and publication. The Dutch, it is true, could be intolerant on occasion, but on the whole their government was extraordinarily broad-minded, and welcomed refugees of every creed and nationality—English fugitives from Laud's Injunctions, Catholics from the Spanish Netherlands, Huguenots from France, Calvinists from Germany and Jews from Spain and Portugal. These foreigners not only paid for shelter with their technical skill, but helped to make Holland the intellectual focus of Europe. Spinoza (1632-1677) was a Portuguese Jew, but he spent his whole life in Amsterdam. He was a pupil of Descartes (1596-1650), who lived for twenty years in Holland and published his most famous work there. Religious and political books unpalatable to Renaissance monarchies appeared with the imprint of Amsterdam or Leyden. To the university of Leyden young men from every part of Europe were sent to finish their education.

[1] *Evelyn's Diary*, Vol. I, p. 26 (1641).

One of the most interesting facts about the Dutch Renaissance is the middle-class soil from which it sprang. Feudal society died early in Holland, and by the seventeenth century both power and wealth were in the hands of the burghers. Their business often gave them wide experience of peoples and customs over half the world, and while opening their minds and sharpening their curiosity, it paid for the luxury of their own cultured lives and enabled them to help the struggling artists and writers of their country and to entertain the cleverest men of Europe. According to Evelyn, the Dutch would readily invest their money in pictures. "It is an ordinary thing," he says, "to find a common farmer lay out two or three thousand pounds on this commodity. Their houses are full of them, and they vend them at their fairs to very great gains."[1]

Contemporary opinion of Holland's greatness was probably less influenced by her intellectual eminence than by her economic success. The spectacle of the wealthy state which monopolized the carrying trade of the world, shared the North Sea fisheries with Great Britain and defended the coveted Spice Islands against all comers, whose sovereignty extended to all the discovered continents of the world, must have offered a staggering contrast to the memory of that "petty province of Holland"[2] which not so long ago had been murmuring against the yoke of Spain and hawking its unwanted allegiance through the courts of Europe.

What most excited the astonishment and envy of contemporaries was the perception that this startling change in the fortunes of a state had an economic and not a political basis. Just as in the Middle Ages all knowledge was part of theology, so, in the early prime of the Renaissance state, were all activities a

---

[1] *Evelyn's Diary*, Vol. I, p. 20.
[2] *Economic Writings of Sir Wm. Petty*. C. H. Hull. Quoted H. F. Russell Smith, *Harrington and His Oceana*, p. 151.

part of politics. And just as long after the Middle Ages were over, philosophy and science could not discard the shadow of their old religious form, so, long after the Renaissance, economic thought was a branch of politics. When Adam Smith lectured in Edinburgh he discussed wealth under the heading of "Police." When in the previous century Sir William Petty wrote a volume on Taxation, he included in his subject liberty of conscience, wars, the Church, the universities, as well as housing, usury and exchange and a score of other economic topics. Yet he followed Harrington in seeing that the true basis of power might be economic rather than political. But it was the Dutch who opened the eyes of the world to this fact. When Petty said that "a small territory and even a few people may, by situation, trade and policy, be made equivalent to a greater, and . . . convenience for shipping and water-carriage do most eminently and fundamentally conduce thereto,"[1] it was the Dutch he had in mind. The French and the Dutch were alike in being mercantilists, but they differed in the details of their economic policy. For the French, economic policy was one among the many constituents of political power. To efficient and centralized administration, a strong army, good frontiers, breadth of territory, a weak nobility and a subservient church, they wanted to add sea-power, manufactures and trade. The Dutch, on the contrary, aimed solely at economic advantages which gave them political weight as a natural result, not as the achievement of direct and deliberate effort. This led them to modify the system of Colbert. Between the two extremes came the English, feeling their way, rather blindly and as though driven by circumstance, to their ultimate reliance on economic development as the true source of political power. The phenomenal success of Holland helped them to understand what they were doing and heart-

[1] Russell Smith, *Harrington and His Oceana*, p. 151.

ened them to continue, but at the same time it made them mistrustful lest they had opened their eyes too late.

The most notable economic changes of the seventeenth century were made in the three fields of industrial invention, of financial experiment and of colonization. In all, Holland stood pre-eminent but not unchallenged. The comparison of Dutch prosperity with their own prompted other states, of which the chief was Great Britain, to imitate what they could not steal of Dutch achievement. " The greatest work in the world, . . ." said Captain John Graunt, " is the making of England as considerable for trade as Holland, for there is but a certain proportion of trade in the world and Holland is prepossessed of the greatest part of it."[1] A generation later, Sir Josiah Child dwelt upon the same theme: " I think," he said, " no true Englishman will deny that the season cries aloud to us to be up and doing . . . before the Dutch get too much the whip-hand of us. . ."[2]

So in many books and pamphlets, English writers of the seventeenth century would break off in their discussion of trade, poor law, currency, or legal reform to probe the causes of Dutch prosperity or to urge the English to copy the Dutch in this way or that. Sir Josiah Child quotes a merchant called Lewis Roberts who had written in the " 'sixties " to show what advantages the Dutch had reaped from their low customs duties. Fabian Phillips, a legal writer of Charles II's time, writes a chapter on "The Fees and Expences in Law, Proceedings in Holland and the Confederate Belgick Provinces."[3] To his thinking, the cause of Dutch prosperity is personal frugality : English luxury is so great that " our Trade must of necessity more and more decay, and will never increase or be advanced,

---

[1] *Observations upon the Bills of Mortality*, 1662.
[2] *A New Discourse of Trade*, p. xli, 1694.
[3] Phillips, *The Reforming Registry*, p. 269 (1671).

if the Dutch were banished out of the world or ordered to trade only in the Bottom of the Sea, and leave all the Surface or Top to us; the cheap diet and clothing of their common people, the neat and frugal diet, and the apparel of the Burgers, and those that they call the Gentry, giving the advantage of underselling us."[1] In his *New Discourse of Trade* (1694) Child defends high wages on the ground that they evidence a nation's wealth, and he proves his point by citing the Dutch who give higher wages than the English by at least 2d. in the shilling. Again, he supports his case for lowering the rate of interest from 6% to 4% by appealing to the experience of Holland, where the low interest of 3% has attracted so great a multitude of merchants "that almost all their People of both sexes are traders."[2] Child gives a depressing list of the trades that Great Britain has lost, entirely or in part, by the close of the seventeenth century. It is the Dutch, he says, who have "beat us out of" nearly all these trades, including the Russian trade, the Greenland trade, the East Country trade, the White Herring trade, the trade for Spanish wools from Bilbao, the East India Spice trade ("an extraordinary profitable trade"), the trade of Scotland and Ireland, the Plate trade from Cadiz, and even the trade of New York, our colony since 1664. In addition they exclude us from their trade with China and Japan, and now that they have taken "Surrenham" (Surinam), "we have no more commerce with that country, then we should if it were sunk in the sea; so severe and exact are the Hollanders, in keeping the trades of their own Plantations intirely to their own People." He attributes Dutch success chiefly to the 3% rate of interest, and says that it is only natural advantages which keep us such trades as we still

---

[1] Phillips, *The Mistaken Recompence* (epistle at end), London, 1664.
[2] Child, *A New Discourse of Trade*, p. xiv (1694).

control. Natural advantages have saved us the Red Herring trade, "otherwise we might say, Farewel, Red-Herrings as well as White"; and it is not our skill but other causes that prevent the Dutch from having a footing in the Newfoundland trade, otherwise "3 per cent would soon send us home to keep sheep." As for the Plantation trades, if it were not for the Navigation Act "you should see forty Dutch ships at our own Plantations for one English."[1] Was ever such a bogey hatched from fear of German trade? Yet Child was no ignorant scaremonger, but one of the best-known men of affairs in the reign of James II.

In the middle of the seventeenth century anyone might have believed that in the realm of overseas dominion the future lay with the Dutch. Holland was gaining in colonial influence at the expense of Spain and Portugal, the old colonial powers, and was still well ahead of the newer maritime powers of England and France. Later on in the century her ruinous wars with England and then with France permanently crippled her chances of expanding into a wide-flung and lasting Empire, but at the time of Charles I's death she seemed, by virtue of her civilization, her wealth, industry and sea-power, to give place to no other nation with the possible exception of France.

Though none of the Dutch towns gained a place so near Evelyn's heart as "sweet Antwerp" over the border, he was much impressed by the evidences of wealth, order and activity that were displayed by the cities of Holland. He tells how "Amsterdam is built and gained upon the main sea, supported by piles at an immense charge, and fitted for the most busy concourse of traffickers and people of commerce beyond any place, or mart, in the world."[2] He speaks of the "extraordinary industry" which pro-

[1] Child, op. cit., pp. xix–xxviii.
[2] *Diary*, I, p. 402 (1641).

vided " this city as generally all the towns of Holland . . . with graffs, cuts, sluices, moles, and rivers," so that one might see " a whole navy of merchants and others environ'd with streets and houses, every man's bark or vessel at anchor before his very door." And then, as if afraid that this might call up a vision of confusion, he adds, "and yet the street so exactly straight, even and uniform, that nothing can be more pleasing, especially being so frequently planted and shaded with the beautiful lime-trees, set in rows before every man's house." He much admired, too, the success of the Dutch in dealing with the problems of poverty and unemployment: " indeed it is most remarkable," he writes, " what provisions are here made and maintain'd for publick and charitable purposes, and to protect the poor from misery, and the country from beggars." Another English writer spoke a little later of the very few beggars in Holland and the great and frequent charity.[1] " De cinq cent mille hommes qui habitent Amsterdam," wrote Voltaire in 1722, " il n'y en a pas un d'oisif, pas un pauvre . . . pas un insolent." He, too, was deeply impressed by the commercial activity of the city " qui est le magasin de l'univers. Il y avait plus de mille vaisseaux dans le port."[2]

In many industrial processes the Dutch set the standard of the West. In the textile industries their dyes were the best; Scotch linen was sent to Holland to be bleached, Holland was the first place where cotton was used in materials, and the linen-thread manufacture of Scotland is said to owe its origin to the theft of Dutch secrets. To establish industries so various as sugar-refining, brass-founding and the running of sawmills Dutch workmen were brought over to England, and the English imitated the Dutch

[1] Capt. John Graunt, *Observations upon the Bills of Mortality*, 1662.
[2] Voltaire, *Les plus belles Lettres*. Ed. Nilsson, p. 9.

in all the ship-building trades. In engineering, too, the Dutch were supreme. Evelyn notes with admiration their harbour works and drainage systems, and when the task of draining the fens in England was seriously undertaken, much of the work was entrusted to the Dutchman Vermuiden to whose name Vermuiden's Dyke is a memorial to this day. Owing to the interest taken by the Dutch in their roads, bridges and waterways, transport was better in Holland than in any other land of the time.

In the country, Holland started modern agriculture and stock-keeping by introducing winter root crops which meant, not only economy of ground, but improvements in the raising of cattle, great numbers of which could now be fed during the winter instead of being slaughtered for salt meat. As gardeners, too, the Dutch were pre-eminent.

As financiers, again, the Dutch led Europe. They were the first to allow the free export of gold and silver, and the first to develop joint-stock enterprise on a large scale. The English banking system was largely copied from the Dutch, as well as financial measures such as the imposition of excises and succession duties.

The unparalleled prosperity and success of the Dutch did not make them personally popular. People of other lands thought them money-grubbing and close-fisted, not without some justification. Their colonial policy, at all events, seems to have been a purely commercial venture, totally lacking the imperial vision of French colonization. Evelyn once dined with the Dutch ambassador who " did in a manner acknowledge that his nation mind only their own profit, do nothing out of gratitude, but collaterally as it relates to their gain or security."[1] They also had their moments of intolerance and fanaticism. But the Dutch ought always to be held in reverence for the generous help they gave to the greatest causes of the seventeenth

[1] *Evelyn's Diary*, May 15, 1659, Vol. I, 333.

century, the cause of liberty and the cause of truth. If at the close of the century England vindicated her old title to a share of the glory, she was then ruled by a Dutch king. Under Charles II and his brother, when the despotism of Louis XIV seemed like to absorb Great Britain and Ireland with the rest of Europe, Holland, not England, was "almost the only spot of ground . . . remaining in the world to publick Liberty."

CHAPTER IV

THE SPIRIT OF MAN

" Without liberty of conscience, civil liberty cannot be perfect ; without civil liberty, liberty of conscience cannot be perfect."
Harrington.

"For it is not the Romane Clergy onely, that pretends the Kingdome of God to be of this world, and thereby to have a Power therein, distinct from that of the Civill State."
Hobbes, Leviathan, 383.

"Now the world is grown saucy and expecteth reasons, and good ones too, before they give up their own opinions to other men's dictates, though never so magisterially delivered to them."
Halifax.

(H. F. Russell Smith, *Religious Liberty under Charles II and James II*, p. 16).

"Descartes n'eût-il fait que substituer des erreurs nouvelles à d'antiques erreurs, c'était déjà un grand bienfait public que d'accoutumer insensiblement les hommes à examiner, et non pas à croire."
Marie-Joseph Chéneri (1792).

MOST inspiration ultimately decays or hardens into the formalism of an organization or school, maintaining existence at the cost of life. As it was with the Christian inspiration which hardened into a Church, so was it with the pagan spontaneity of the Renaissance which crystallized into the rigid perfection of Louis XIV's despotism, the artificial gardens of Versailles, the "faultily faultless" prose of Boileau, the inviolate satisfaction of the age with the methods and achievements of the ancient world. On the other hand, the Renaissance triumphed not in consolidation only, but also in new inspiration.

The seventeenth century registered the claims of individual freedom in thought, in worship and in citizenship : it fulfilled the scientific promise of Da Vinci's day and foreshadowed the economic expansion of our own.

As usual, there was often hostility between the forces of organization and the forces of freedom, but sometimes there was alliance. And sometimes out of organization came inspiration, as when the attempt to reproduce the drama of Greece proved the starting-point of modern opera. France and Holland roughly symbolize the division of forces. Their political hostility was the obverse of intellectual antipathy. The government of France under Louis XIV was the greatest triumph of the Renaissance state. The literature of his reign was a golden-tongued witness to the triumph of the classical authors raised from the dead by the Revival of Learning. Holland stood rather for the free development of personality. Her government refused to subscribe to the Renaissance model. Intellectually she stood for freedom of thought in science and religion. Economically she was the pioneer of the Western world in financial and industrial experiment. But just as there was sometimes a connection between the forces of organization and those of inspiration, so France, in spite of her government, took a memorable share in producing the independent thought of the day, as she also rivalled Holland in economic expansion overseas. On the other hand, Holland's commercial policy lacked the germs of liberality present in the English system, and Dutch colonial expansion was wholly lacking in the imperial breadth of view that inspired the colonial ventures of France.

In its century of triumph, the Renaissance lost not only spontaneity and freedom, but universality. Spain in the beginning of her slow decline deeply influenced the drama of France and England, and Italian influences were felt in the theatres and musical circles of France, but with few exceptions all that was most vital in the civilization of the seventeenth century came from three countries only—France, England and Holland. The other countries of Europe were imitators before all else : most of them copied the inventions of Holland, and they all tried, sometimes with ludicrous results, to reproduce the culture of France.

If France was the heir of Renaissance political ideals, she was also heir to the revival of learning. Seventeenth century literature had two main characteristics : first an intellectual and objective outlook and secondly its classical form, and it was in French literature that both these characteristics were most pronounced. The former was in part due to the preoccupation of the best minds of the day with the search for knowledge and with the explanation of scientific phenomena, but it was in part a heritage from the Latin classics. When Boileau (1636-1711), the critic of the age, defines the aim of French writers he says :—

" Quelque sujet qu'on traite, ou plaisant, ou sublime,
Que toujours le bon sens s'accorde avec la rime

. . . . . .

Aimez donc la raison—que toujours vos écrits
Empruntent d'elle seule et leur lustre et leur prix."[1]

And again he explains what he means by a good play :—

" J'aime sur le théâtre un agréable auteur
Qui . . .
Plait par la raison seule."[2]

Corneille's heroes and heroines are like disembodied intellects of ruthless power, forging colossal chains of thought by a detached and inhuman logic.[3] Racine, whose glory it was to crown French drama with his own

[1] *L'Art Poètique*, Chant premier.
[2] *Ib.*, Chant III.
[3] Lytton Strachey, *Landmarks in French Literature*, p. 53.

genius, did interpret the emotions of men and women. But if Corneille (1606-1684) made intellect a passion, Racine (1639-1699) made passion intellectual, almost objective. In prose again, intellectual force was predominant. Pascal (1623-1662) put French prose into the crucible of his own intellect and drew forth the most perfect instrument that human reason has ever employed—clear, logical and concise, and, what is still more wonderful, as readable as it is accurate.

Much of the English literature of the day has something of this intellectual and impersonal outlook. In *Paradise Lost*, Milton (1608-1674) prays for illumination

> "That to the heighth of this great *argument*
> I may assert Eternal Providence
> And justify the ways of God to men."

And whether he intended it or not, for many of his readers he has made Satan stand for all time as the type of intellect baffled by force, yet asserting

> "that he . . . who overcomes by force, hath overcome but half his foe."

Much even of the love-poetry seems impersonal,—designed to show a pretty wit or clever turn of phrase rather than to express an overpowering emotion. To turn from Marvell's

> "Had we but world enough and time,"

to Shakespeare's sonnet,

> "Then hate me when thou wilt,"

is to see this at once.

In form, English prose and poetry were quickly influenced by the revival of learning, but the full effects of the movement were not felt till the seventeenth century. Superficially the influence of the classics was evident in a changed vocabulary and setting. From Milton, classical names fall "thick as autumnal leaves that strew the brooks in Vallombrosa "; in parts of *Comus* almost every line has a classical allusion. A sentence chosen at random from Sir Thomas Browne's books is likely to contain more Latin words than English. An argument, too, was felt to be strengthened if it could be supported by classical example or precept. " Do ye beleeve me yet," says the elder brother in *Comus*, " or shall I call antiquity from the old schools of Greece ? " Economic writers such as Child and Davenant, especially the latter, appealed to Roman and Greek experience ; and even the mystic poets of England, in many ways alien to the Renaissance spirit, did not escape the fascination of classical literature nor free their own from its influence.

The seventeenth century had also a purely Latin literature of its own. Milton would write Latin prose or poetry, and it was in Latin that Grotius wrote his history of the Netherlands revolt. He, too, wrote Latin poems, and Thomas Hobbes wrote his autobiography in Latin elegiac verse.

But seventeenth century writers did not merely imitate. This was the greatest age of Dutch literature, and English seventeenth century prose has seldom, if ever, been surpassed. In its dignity, its directness, and its terse self-control, it not only succeeded in recapturing something of the quality of its great models but created an independent beauty of its own.

This is equally true of the French drama. In France, not only the form but the whole nature of literary creation was transformed by the classical tradition. It was not enough that Corneille and Racine should usually choose classical themes, but they must also build their plays on the Senecan model. Accordingly, concentration came to be the watchword of the French "classical" writers, who bound themselves, by Aristotle's famous " unities " of time, place and action, not to admit into their work any distraction or irrelevancy that might mar the perfect lucidity of their central idea. So in Racine's plays we get one problem attacked, few people involved, scarcely any background given, the minimum of movement allowed.

At a first reading of Racine's plays, the perfect symmetry of arrangement is more striking than anything else. Take *Andromaque*. The *dramatis personæ* are only eight—two men and two women, each with a "confidante." The single theme is the conflict which consumes the leading figures—a conflict between personal passion and common sense. They are finally mastered by passion, while the confidantes all urge the losing cause of common sense. As the tragedy unrolls, each of the four principal actors illuminates a different aspect of the one problem. In Pyrrhus the common sense of kingly dignity, of public and private loyalty, contends with his infatuation for Andromaque. Hermione's passion for Pyrrhus, alternating with hate and shot with jealousy, tramples under-foot the common sense of safety and personal dignity, and finally destroys both Pyrrhus and herself. Reason and good faith demand from Oreste an indifference to Hermione that he can neither feel nor show: to him passion seems a tyrant which, after repeated rebellion, he comes almost to revere as fate. For Andromaque herself the struggle is still more bitter. Common sense and mother-love join issue in her heart with the religious passion of her loyalty to her dead husband, and sooner than allow the mastery of either claim she resolves to save her son and then to kill herself.

To cut out a scene, to omit the part of the humblest actor in the play would be impossible, so close is the interweaving of the drama, so essential the action of the slightest figure introduced. This could not be said of Shakespeare's work.[1] The impossibility of taking

[1] Could it be said even of Ibsen's plays, short and sparsely peopled as they often are? Leave only four people in *A Doll's House*, and four in *Hedda Gabler*, take away everyone but Hilda and Solness from the *Master Builder* and you still have the essence of the plays.

out a single figure from Racine's plays has a necessary corollary. If the play cannot live without the people neither can the people live without the play. This is condemned by lovers of Shakespeare who like to think of Cordelia and Hamlet apart from the plays, and to recognize Falstaff and Malvolio in the streets. It is possible to do this because Shakespeare's people seem to inhabit their plays. We watch them pass through a certain phase of experience which leads them from a past and often to a future which we cannot share, but which are nevertheless real. Racine's people do not pass through their plays, because they are the plays. They are not inhuman or unreal. Every line they say, every feeling they express, is true to human experience—not to the unpurged gross of everyday emotion, but to its essential core laid bare by crisis. Their love or hate does not leap in flame from year to year, from land to land. Four walls and a few hours confine the passion of Titus and Bérénice, and maybe help to keep its glow at white heat. This concentrated emotion, under pressure of time and space, makes them seem unreal, because we do not meet people who can live for half a day at the unflagging tensity of emotional strength or weakness of Racine's godlike creatures. While the play lasts they are strangely real; when it is over they become glorious possibilities.

None but his compatriots can hope to drink the full perfection of Racine's verse. Yet who that has heard them echo through a French theatre can forget the passionate restraint of the lines:—

> "Songe, songe, Céphise à cette nuit cruelle
> Qui fut pour tout un peuple une nuit éternelle,"

with the lingering sadness of their soft consonants and the long-drawn grief of the vowels, pierced by the sharp " t " or " q "? Such lines are not rare in Racine. He was supreme not so much because he could write perfect lines but because he could scarcely write anything else.

And the constant worship of his countrymen from his own day to ours is proof that this perfection is not a thing of passing fancy. Shakespeare has had his day of eclipse with us; Racine never with the French.[1] To-day it is often impossible to see Shakespeare acted in London, but it would be hard to spend ten days in Paris without the chance of seeing one of the masterpieces of Racine. In the eighteenth century Mme. du Deffand and Diderot said in the fashion of their own age what Anatole France has said in ours: " O doux et grand Racine ! . . . Corneille n'est près de vous qu'un habile déclamateur, et je ne sais si Molière luimême est aussi vrai que vous, ô maître souverain, en qui réside toute verité et toute beauté . . . je ne veux pas mourrir sans avoir écrit quelques lignes au pied de votre monument, ô Jean Racine, en temoignage de mon amour et de ma piété."[2]

Molière (1620-1673), it is true, allowed himself more freedom than Racine, but he was none the less master of that concentration which makes his work so different from the all-embracing plays of Shakespeare. It needed, however, the genius of a La Fontaine or a Molière to produce perfection in such rigid limits. In lesser hands, the classical tradition became sterile : in their allegiance to antiquity, writers were led away from the spirit of their models by the lure of their form. They did not seek new inspiration from the artist's spirit : what they wanted was to reproduce the form of his creation. In this they might succeed, but where imitation is substituted for invention, poetry is dead.

But in Racine's day, the best literature of the time had a vital individuality. So long as the intellectual and social leaders of French society lived the polished life of " ordered beauty " of which the name of France conjured a vision to the envious mind of seventeenth century Europe, so long was the rarefied atmosphere

---

[1] Apart from the momentary jealousies of his own day.
[2] Anatole France, *Le Petit Pierre*, pp. 330–331 (Calmann Levy).

of French classical literature a true expression of a nationality which was none the less real because it was clothed in ceremony and walked in gardens of fantastic trimness.

It was when the classical tradition of Corneille and Racine came to bind the whole of Europe, when every literary production teemed with senseless classical allusions, when some were peopled with pagan gods, when others adopted the pastoral model of Theocritus to describe the condition of contemporary peasants, when Homer was voted barbaric and Virgil was praised for his polish, when Gothic architecture was the despair of good taste and when good Germans became bad Frenchmen—it was then that the dead hand of antiquity fell heavy upon art. This happened in the eighteenth century.

In the seventeenth century, however, classical antiquity was, like the Bible, an armoury for rival thinkers. La Fontaine and Racine drew from it the polished rapiers that lent a glitter to Louis XIV's despotism, but the commonwealth men of England found there many a stout cudgel for chastizing monarchy on behalf of law.

On the whole, in pre-Renaissance days, the memory of Roman times had served the cause of absolute government, because to mediæval Europe Rome had meant imperial Rome, and knowledge of Rome meant knowledge of Roman law as codified under the Empire. But the Revival of Learning, with a truer sense of historical values, emphasized the importance of the older and more creative republican times, when government, however oligarchic in fact, was based on democratic principles. Again, while from a modern point of view most Greek governments seem to have been oligarchies or aristocracies in practice, the majority of them were democratic in theory and in the forms of their constitutions.

Thomas Hobbes (1588-1679), who as a true successor

to Machiavelli brought his best gifts to the support of efficient despotism,[1] saw what danger to absolute government lurked in the study of the classics. Young men entered public life, having read at the universities " the glorious histories and sententious politics of the ancient popular governments of the Greeks and Romans, amongst whom Kings were branded with the names of tyrants and popular governments . . . passed by the name of liberty."[2] In France the younger members of the Parlement, when making their demands of the monarchy in 1648, compared themselves to Roman senators.

It was the study of the classics, too, that helped to give to the anti-monarchical tendencies of the seventeenth century their peculiar republican and legal cast. Unlike the democrats of the eighteenth and nineteenth centuries, the seventeenth century advocates of liberty did not believe in the practical sovereignty of men. They agreed with their enemy Hobbes in thinking that " nothing is more easily broken than a man's word " and that the " Passions of men are commonly more potent than their reason." Harrington, the English revolutionary (1611-1677), might approach the doctrine of the " general will," but his hopes were set upon the government of laws, not of men.

This last infirmity of seventeenth century thought, this demand for a " somewhat fundamental "[3] out of reach of personal interests and momentary desires, persisted with equal force in the next century. Side by side with faith in human reason went faith in the virtue of laws. Not all the failure of enlightened despotism, not all their own experience of administration could free the minds of Robespierre and his

[1] " The obligation of subjects to the sovereign is understood to last as long and no longer than the power lasteth by which he is able to protect them " (Hobbes).
[2] Hobbes, *Behemoth*, 428, quoted Russell Smith, *Harrington and His Oceana*, p. 16.
[3] Cromwell, *Speech to First Protectorate Parliament*, 12 Sept., 1654.

followers from the empery of this belief. Plutarch must bear some indirect responsibility for this because of the great influence of his *Lycurgus*. " Here was a man who made laws and institutions in his own head and imposed them upon his fellow-countrymen. So Plutarch wrote and believed, and so read and believed thinking Frenchmen of the eighteenth century."[1]

We may laugh at this pathetic faith in general, and in particular at seventeenth century misunderstandings of Magna Carta, or point to the failure of the Instrument of Government. We may think Cromwell more unconstitutional than Charles I; we may urge the absolutism of Charles II as a proof of the Puritan failure. All the same, the Puritans won the real victory because they prevented the principle that the king's will has necessarily the force of law from taking root in England. At the time, they merely substituted one tyranny for another, but in the long run the difference between Royalists and Puritans is fundamentally the same as the difference which separates America and the self-governing parts of the British Empire from most other states ; that is, the difference which separates the " rule of law " from " droit administratif." In Anglo-Saxon countries, administrators and citizens are subject to one law, and they are responsible to the same courts ; in continental countries there is one law for administrators, another for citizens ; one kind of court for administrators, another for citizens. In Anglo-Saxon states the police exist for the protection of citizens: in continental countries they exist to spy on them.[2]

This fundamental difference between the two types of state had been developing for centuries. Every state had the two opposing principles within its bosom :

[1] T. R. Glover, *The Conflict of Religions in the Early Roman Empire*, p. 84.
[2] Anglo-Saxon countries have been approaching the "droit administratif" model lately, especially since 1914, but it is possible that the change is merely temporary.

both were implicit in the theory of the feudal system, and the Church with its idea of a law above the king had struggled with the imperial idea that the king's will has the force of law. And all the while the conflict of principles was the reflection of a conflict of material forces. In England, owing to various peculiarities in legal and constitutional history, the conflict had not died down, but was merely quiescent, under the New Monarchy of the Tudors. But because there was a real danger in Stuart times that England, like the rest of Europe, would follow the administrative and legal model perfected in France under Louis XIV, and because the Puritans and their successors, the Whigs of 1688, prevented their country from doing so, it seems just to place the definite parting of the ways in the seventeenth century.

The idea that kingship was derived from and therefore subject to law was vindicated in England not only by the destructive methods of rebellion and debate but by a constructive attempt to govern by written constitutions. It was felt that only where the letter of the rules of government was written down in black and white was there any security from the never-ending audacity of the royal prerogative, whose trespasses on the debatable ground of the constitution had too often proved not only successful but technically justifiable. Long before it came to fighting, Charles I's opponents complained that " The root of all this mischief we find to be a malignant and pernicious design of subverting the *fundamental laws and principles of government* upon which the religion and justice of this kingdom are finally established."[1] That was why the seventeenth century lawyers made the fame of Magna Carta; why attempts were made to govern England by three successive written constitutions, the Agreement of the People (1648), the Instru-

[1] Grand Remonstrance. See Gardiner, *The Constitutional Documents of the Puritan Revolution*, 3rd Edition, p. 202.

ment of Government (1653) and the Humble Petition and Advice (1657). Each of these constitutions was fundamentally different from the others because no two of them agreed on the vital question of who was to be sovereign—whether legislature, executive or a mixture of both. Each of them in turn broke down. None was a safeguard against tyranny: none was a guarantee of the rule of law, any more than are the written constitutions of to-day. But they proved the strength of a desire to limit autocracy in the very hour of its triumph, and it is at least probable that they, or rather the political principle which gave them birth, helped to shape the constitutions of some American states, to determine later the peculiar rigidity and sovereign position of the Federal constitution of the United States, and even to swell the flood of written constitutions that threatened to submerge the autocracies of the nineteenth century. It has to be remembered, however, that the idea of a written constitution could not be strange in America where several of the states had been governed under written charters from the days of their foundation; and again, that for a federal state a written constitution is in the first place a practical necessity, and only secondarily, if at all, the expression of a political ideal.

Two theories, both of a legal nature, both of a classical ancestry, justified the limitation of monarchy. One was the theory of the contractual basis of the state; the other was the theory of natural law.

The belief that each state was founded by a contract had not been forgotten in the Middle Ages, but it was given a new and more active lease of life by the Revival of Learning. According to the most usual form of this doctrine, states had been created by an agreement between people and ruler. If the ruler broke the terms of this agreement the people had a right to rebel. Hobbes stole this democratic weapon for absolute monarchy by maintaining that the agreement had been made among the people themselves, who, for the sake of security, had put their power into the hands of the ruler. He could not break an agreement to which he was not a party, so that unless he endangered his subjects' security by inefficiency, he could not forfeit his power. Charles II perhaps realized more closely than anyone else Hobbes's conception of a ruler. On the one hand he owed his power to an agreement made by his future subjects; on the other that power was given him almost unconditionally. On the one hand, he was never able completely to substitute for kingship by the subjects' will kingship by Divine Right—an idea which must have seemed to Hobbes to come from where " there walketh . . . as it were a kingdom of Fayries, in the dark . . ." —on the other hand, he nearly realized Hobbes's ideal of absolute government. But Hobbes could not prevent the Parliamentarians from taking back the contract weapon. The Whigs justified the deposition of James II by claiming that he had broken the original compact by virtue of which he had ruled, just as Milton before them had justified the execution of Charles I on the same ground. William III was a contract-king in Locke's sense. He owed his crown to an agreement made between himself and his future subjects. If he broke that agreement they would be under no obligation to obey him. And as the Bill of Rights limited the kingship of William III, so did the Act of Settlement limit the kingship of George I.

The second theory, that of natural law, was wider in meaning and in application than the social contract idea. By the seventeenth century, the Stoic doctrine of the law of nature had been confounded with the later Roman idea of a law of nations and with the Christian idea of Divine Law. Law was still to the seventeenth century what it had been to the Greeks and to the Middle Ages—something immutable and eternal, not to be made, but to be discovered and interpreted by men. It was the hidden figure in the rough block, awaiting the chisel of a Michael Angelo to free it from the encasing marble and reveal its beauty to the world. In essence this figure was the embodiment of human reason. Its message was threefold: first to man as a human being living in a material world, next to man as an immortal soul with hopes of heaven, and thirdly to man as a member of society. Put in another way, this means that the business of a righteous ruler was to preserve men's bodies and their property and to uphold religion and morality. Statute law and case law ought to be redactions of the unwritten law of nature and to provide punishment for disobedience to it. Where no appeal could be made to positive law, this unwritten law of nature must govern conduct; for instance if a man falls among thieves and takes a false oath in order to preserve himself, it is to the law of nature that he must appeal for justification.

The revived study of antiquity increased the influence of the "law of nature," and as might be expected, the effect of this influence was to limit, however meagrely, the unbridled will of Renaissance despots. The idea of natural law limited the power of kings at home because it helped the twin causes of civic and religious liberty: it claimed a voice in their policy abroad because it was the inspiration of international law.

The relations between states were not governed by positive law; therefore, it had long been felt, they must be referred to natural law. Such a conviction had small practical importance before the age of sovereign states. But in the sixteenth and seventeenth centuries, when Pope and Emperor were discredited, and the Machiavellian states were fighting with uncontrolled licence, it became necessary, not so much in the interests of humanity, perhaps, as in the interests of governments themselves, that national rights and duties should be defined, either by some powerful arbitrator or by a code of rules acceptable to all.

From the fourteenth century onwards, schemes had been hatched, chiefly by French thinkers, to replace Pope and Emperor by European peace-leagues which, usually under the ægis of France, were to control international relations. But though, in the history of thought, the modern League of Nations is the descendant of these schemes, they were all abortive at the time.

Far more fruitful was the code of rules drawn up by Hugo Grotius (1583-1645). He brought to earth the divine but nebulous law of nature and made it fit for common use. In his *De Jure Belli ac Pacis* (1625) he wrote down this unwritten law, and built upon it a guide for the conduct of nations in peace and war. This might have been a purely academic performance. But Grotius was not only a lawyer and a scholar: he was a diplomat and politician as well, and he knew the men and manners of at least two countries beside his own. And because his point of view was practical and for the most part acceptable to his generation, his version of the law of nature was felt to be authoritative. Such commonly conceived rights and duties as self-preservation and the obligation to keep promises were the foundation of his " law of nations," though he built into it parts of Roman Law as well as the written conventions and accepted customs which did to some extent, even in and before his day, control the relations of states.

In a sense his outlook was partly mediæval, for like Althusius, he considered states to be members of a society, not, like Machiavelli, as isolated communities surrounded by implacable enemies. But for the most part he was essentially modern. In the first place he never thought of states as members of a peaceful and united Christendom; he recognized the likelihood of frequent quarrels among them, and aimed, not to prevent them from fighting, but to persuade them to fight according to accepted rules, and not like Machiavelli's lions and foxes. In the second place he definitely accepted the Renaissance polity. He did not contemplate a Pope or an Emperor who would enforce the rules of war and peace. He was concerned throughout with the sovereign, territorial state which had no superior. This acceptance of Renaissance political theory prevented him from accepting one of the chief political facts of his age, that is the Cæsarism by which each large state strove to absorb its smaller neighbours. In his eyes, each state, whether large or small, was of equal and sovereign status, each was a legal person. This notion, too, was acceptable to all save the most powerful of states, and would scarcely be openly condemned by them.

It was this essentially modern outlook, combined with the need of rules for international affairs, that made the work of Grotius famous, immediately and for ever. It passed through more than forty-five editions, and though the international lawyers of to-day believe no longer in the law of nature, their work undoubtedly rests at bottom on the foundation that Grotius laid.

Three years after he died, the Peace of Westphalia (1648) showed that Europe was, in form as well as in substance, the society of sovereign states with divergent interests that he had envisaged. There was not even the pretence of a Christian commonwealth with single aim and dual head. Catholics and Protestants, it is true, met in different places, but either at Münster or Osnabrück all the greater governments of Europe, except England, Poland and Russia, were represented, as well as most of the smaller states. For the first time in history the affairs of Europe were settled by a conference of European states meeting as equals. The Pope was represented, but even the theory of his joint supremacy with the Emperor was abandoned, while the latter was weakened by the practical recognition of the independence of the German princes. The principle of state sovereignty was upheld when the independence of Holland and Switzerland—both small states and both republics in an age of monarchy—was formally recognized. Grotius himself had contemplated the inclusion of Turkey in the councils of Europe, but it was not until the nineteenth century that the Turks were invited to a European conference, although the French had close diplomatic and commercial relations with them from the sixteenth century onwards.

The rules that Grotius laid down were violated often enough, but they were not thereby discredited. Nobody could have betrayed the principles of international law more often than Louis XIV, but he always thought it necessary to produce legal justification for his aggressions. Lip-service is not useless if it be lasting : it can save an ideal from oblivion, and International Law may fitly hope to command public opinion since public opinion has never ceased to commend it.

Because it gave a man the right to preserve himself and his property, natural law usually implied claims on the part of the individual as against the government. But the law of nature was not necessarily a rebel's creed. Absolutists like Hobbes believed in it as firmly as republicans like Harrington. Hobbes, it is true, can be accused of deriving ethics from politics, of maintaining that outside civil society there is no such thing as right or wrong, yet this is what he says of natural law: "Princes succeed one another: and one judge passeth, another cometh ; nay heaven and earth shall pass ; but not one tittle of the Law of Nature shall pass : for it is the eternal law of God." He expressly says, however, that where there is a conflict between natural law and the fiat of the sovereign, the sovereign must be obeyed. To him there was no dilemma. Self-preservation was the foremost precept of natural law, and a sovereign who ceased to minister to his subjects' preservation ceased, in his view, to be sovereign. But to us it seems that he placed security above law. It was when people placed law above everything else that the doctrine of natural law became revolutionary. Again, who was to interpret the law of nature ? The Levellers, who went beyond republicanism to democracy, held the individual conscience to be sole arbiter. This made Cromwell think that a belief in natural law might be carried too far.

As applied to religion, the law of nature again threatened the omnipotence of kings, because, within certain limits, it implied the right to freedom of worship. According to the law of nature, toleration was not a universal natural right ; neither atheists nor people who practised unnatural ceremonies nor those who substituted authority for reason ought to be tolerated, but all those who based their religion on reason had a right to exercise their beliefs.

This close connection in theory between civil and religious freedom was a reflection of political facts. As we saw earlier, in any state where the Church was a department of secular government or where secular government was a department of the Church, difference of belief was treason. That is, freedom of belief was a political offence. In any state whatsoever, strong government was bound to aim at the control of belief as it aimed at the control of everything else. The Roundheads fought for civil and religious liberty, but when they won the victory they were not disposed to grant either. But what made the assertion of religious freedom so helpful to the cause of civil liberty was the fact that, on the whole, people minded more about the free exercise of their religion than they minded about the free exercise of anything else, except their money. In the Great Rebellion there was a constitutional problem, a military problem and a religious problem, but it was the religious problem that forced the issue—that gave Charles I a party and a cause, that gave the Roundheads their army and their leaders.

There were two distinct kinds of religious freedom. There was the freedom of the individual, and the freedom of his group. On the whole the first kind, as being less likely to pass into definite political opposition to the state, was more lightly granted than the second. Again, there were many degrees of religious freedom for individuals, all determined by political motives. For instance, though it might be thought safe in a Protestant state that a man should attend Mass, it might not be thought safe that he should be an ambassador or that he should be allowed to teach children.

There were, too, many different ways of looking at toleration, and consequently many different ways of getting it. Though the Reformation sprang from the will to have individual liberty in religion, the movement gave birth to religious freedom only in spite of itself. Luther was not tolerant. Calvinist iconoclasm in Holland and cruelty in Geneva no less than Puritan narrowmindedness in England proved that any religious body might become intolerant with opportunity. According to Cromwell, "Every sect saith 'oh, give me liberty.' But give it to him, and to his power he will not yield it to anybody else."[1] "Holy Men," said John Cleveland, "like the Holy Language must be read backwards. They rifle Colleges to promote Learning, and pull down Churches for Edification."[2] But once the ancient Church had split, division was hydra-headed, each serpent-mouth hissing at other. With division of faiths went division of power, and when at length no one sect could overbear the rest, the situation became perforce one of "live and let live."

The governmental point of view was different.

[1] Cromwell, *Letters and Speeches*, 12 Sept., 1654 (Carlyle).
[2] Quoted *The Eagle*, June, 1919, p. 166.

Kings did not look upon religious liberty as the logical consequence of a sullen deadlock. They thought it a matter of grace, or as the Stuarts put it, of "indulgence." In England, Charles II and James II hoped to gain toleration for their Catholic friends if they gave it to the Nonconformists. In France, the king gave and the king took away. In Prussia, where religious liberty was more complete than in any other country save Holland, the Calvinist Hohenzollerns allowed their subjects to remain Lutheran.

From yet a third point of view, toleration was a matter of right not of grace, a thing to be taken if necessary by force, not to be received as a gift. This standpoint was adopted by the Jesuits on the one hand, and on the other by the Independents in England. The Independents argued mainly on behalf of individual liberty of worship, the Jesuits on behalf of the rights of a group. They were working for their own group only, but in claiming that the Church was a "perfect society" separate from the other "perfect society" of the state, they appealed to principles which could be used to support the claims of all other groups to possess an independent life of their own, not derived from the life of the state.

Of more immediate effect was the idea that toleration was a matter of expediency. In the early days of British colonization in America, English rulers were not blind to this point of view. Though to satisfy opinion at home they withheld formal recognition of dissent, they tacitly allowed it to exist in America in order to create a safety-valve for religious feeling. When in 1629 the Massachusetts Bay Company received its charter, no reference was made to conformity with the Church of England. Four years later, it is true, Massachusetts was arraigned before the Privy Council partly on account of its divergence from Anglicanism, but, when the proceedings were over, it appeared " that his Majesty did not intend to impose the ceremonies of the Church of England upon us; for that it was considered that it was our freedom from such things that made people come over to us; and it was credibly informed to the Council that this country would, in time, be very beneficial to England for masts, cordage, etc., if the Sound should be debarred."[1] A year before this the grant of a charter to Lord Baltimore, well known to be a Catholic, was a practical sanction to the establishment of the Romish faith in Maryland. A generation later Rhode Island received a charter with complete toleration.

After a chequered career under the patronage of the Stuarts and also of the Levellers, the cause of religious liberty in England was championed by the Whig aristocracy. The Whig was not an idealist. He had two gods—property and the constitution. Personal safety depended on a right worship of these two. To him, as to his philosopher Locke, the state existed to protect property: its business "is to preserve men's bodies and not to save their souls." The good behaviour of the Nonconformists during the Popish panic strengthened this view, which was well expressed in 1687 by a letter from a gentleman in the country to his friend in London. "Does his going to a conventicle naturally qualify (a man) for a constable's staff? Or believing Transubstantiation render him incapable of being a good clerk? It were as reasonable to say that 'tis impossible for a fanatic to be a good shoemaker or a papist a good tailor."[2] Toleration, then, was common sense. This does not mean that all religious bodies were treated alike. Freedom of worship did not mean equality of privilege. England was behind Prussia and Holland in this respect: English Papists had long to wait before they had equal privileges with the Protestant Nonconformists, and

---

[1] Egerton, *British Colonial Policy*, p. 46.
[2] H. F. Russell Smith, *The Theory of Religious Liberty in the Reigns of Charles II and James II*, 1911, p. 41.

it was not until our own day that religious tests for certain offices were finally abolished. What is more, Prussia, Holland and England were the only countries where religious beliefs were free. In the Roman Catholic countries injustice and persecution were often the lot of the unorthodox throughout the greater part of the eighteenth century.

Nevertheless, it is clear that in the seventeenth century people were getting used to the idea that religious beliefs might be safely and wisely left to personal choice. Englishmen like William Penn and Sir Thomas Browne thought freedom of conscience a simple dictate of common sense. Sir Thomas said he could not " fall out, or contemn a man for an errour or conceive why a difference in opinion should divide an affection: For . . . there remains not many controversies worth a Passion." According to Penn, " a man may be a very good Englishman and yet a very indifferent churchman," while Milton saw positive advantages in varieties of religious belief. " Out of the many moderate varieties and brotherly dissimilitudes that are not vastly disproportional," he wrote, "arises the godly and graceful symmetry that commands the whole pile and structure."[1] Even in Catholic France two well-known men of widely differing points of view argued in favour of toleration. One was the ardent Catholic Fénélon and the other the extreme sceptic Bayle.

The general desire to solve the religious problem in a reasonable way was chiefly due to the emancipation of mind achieved by a revolution in thought which was foreshadowed in the early years of the Renaissance, but which was not triumphant till the seventeenth century. Of this movement Bacon was the prophet (1561-1626), Descartes the preacher (1596-1650), and Newton the product (1642-1727).

The Revival of Learning had in some ways stunted

[1] H. F. Russell Smith, op. cit., p. 11.

the development of scientific thought and discovery. People were so dazzled by the achievements of the Greeks that they merely studied ancient methods of research without trying to evolve something new for themselves. They felt that humanity had declined since the great days of Greece and that there was nothing left to do but to copy the past as faithfully as possible. On these lines little progress could be made, for except in geometry the Greeks made little advance in mathematics. But other people thought that the great geographical discoveries of the sixteenth century, its inventions, its achievements in art and literature, entitled their age to take a more cheerful view of its own powers. In France, the two forces of " Ancients " and " Moderns "[1] joined issue in a long and wordy battle whose echoes resounded in English coffee-houses towards the close of the seventeenth century. Now that the last signs of the conflict are thickly overlaid with library dust we can see that whether the seventeenth century fell behind the Greeks in literature or not, it clearly surpassed them in scientific achievement.

The seventeenth century revolution in thought was a different thing from the physical and mathematical discoveries connected with it. It was a revolution in point of view and in method. The point of view of pre-Baconian thought was the point of view of the Church. In the first place, all branches of thought were countenanced only if they appeared to minister to theology. Secondly, and consequently, any theory that contradicted the accepted teaching of theology was heretical and therefore untrue. Thirdly, any conclusion that might be drawn about nature was held to be of little use because at any time it might be made invalid by the miraculous intervention of Providence. Fourthly, it was thought a waste of time to interest oneself in terrestrial phenomena for their own sake because

[1] See Molière, *Le Mariage Forcé*.

this life was merely a cold and noisome ante-room to the next world. Last, but not least, the Church emphasized its point of view in the most practical way possible by the use of imprisonment, torture and the stake. The method of pre-Baconian thought was the method of Aristotle—that is, not the experimental method which Aristotle employs in the *Politics*, a book which seems to have had little influence on mediæval thought,[1] but the method of his formal logic. According to this method of thinking, the thinker starts with a preconceived notion—such as, for instance, the notion that the earth is the mainspring and centre of the universe—and goes on to draw from it conclusions which he takes to be true provided that he has obtained them without breaking any of the rules of logic. This way of thinking, however perverse it seems, was the only way possible for the vast majority of mediæval churchmen, who, believing that the voice of the Scriptures and of ecclesiastical tradition was the voice of God, could not but choose to take for truth the whole body of preconceived ideas so presented to them.

Hobbes, who cheerfully called the Church "the Kingdom of Darknesse," summed up the situation in his own inimitable if prejudiced fashion. "And for the study of Philosophy," he says, "it hath no otherwise place, then as a handmaid to the Romane Religion: and since the authority of Aristotle is onely current there, that study is not properly Philosophy (the nature whereof dependeth not on authors) but Aristotelity. And for Geometry, till of very late times it had no place at all; as being subservient to nothing but rigide Truth. And if any man by the ingenuity of his owne nature, had attained to any degree of perfection therein, hee was commonly thought a Magician, and his Art Diabolicall."[2]

[1] It was used, however, by Aquinas and by Marsilius of Padua.
[2] *Leviathan*, c. 46.

Francis Bacon's work was to show the possibility of looking on knowledge from a different point of view. One of the main impulses in the æsthetic Renaissance of Italy had been the conviction that human life as lived on this earth is beautiful and good in and for itself. It was from this point of view that Bacon looked on knowledge. Knowledge is not needed to prepare men for a future life but to help them in this world. Science must aim at "the endowment of human life with new inventions and riches,"[1] it must give to man the control of the forces of nature.

But it is impossible to control nature without understanding it. Bacon saw that such understanding could come only from direct examination. Therefore he regarded experience, and not authority, as the sole source of truth. In his ideal country of "Atlantis" the most important institution was not the Church, but the college of scientific investigators.

Bacon did not altogether live up to his ideas. On the authority of tradition he believed in astrology and in the old earth-centring idea of the universe. So perhaps it is not wonderful that his point of view and method were not widely spread in his own time: he was "light, not fire."[2] But his light was caught up, made clearer and diffused more widely by Descartes.

Descartes went further than Bacon in distrust of authority and tradition. So far was he from reverencing the past that he repudiated all his debts to it. His greatness rests on two achievements, his mathematical discoveries and his contributions to the Baconian method of thinking. He did for philosophical thought what Bacon had done for the study of natural phenomena. The problems of philosophy are not capable of solution by the rough-and-ready methods of experience which still have to satisfy scientists. Scientists, for instance, appear to assume that the plants

---

[1] Bury, *Idea of Progress*, p. 52.
[2] E. Sichel, *The Renaissance*, p. 193.

and animals, gases and metals which they study have an objective reality. Philosophers do not want to assume anything. But they must start from something. So Descartes found, when he had put on one side all the traditional ideas from which mediæval philosophers had started. In their stead, as was natural for a mathematician, he put a quasi-mathematical idea. It seemed to him that geometrical axioms which were recognizable by every man independently of experience, and which were therefore incapable of proof, must be true. Descartes thought he had found an axiomatic truth of this sort in the statement " I think, therefore I am." He took that axiom as a starting-point, and then aimed at doubting everything to start with, accepting nothing because it was believed by others, and believing a thing to be true only where doubt seemed impossible. This means that a man's reason is the sole test of truth.

There is not much of Descartes' philosophy standing to-day. He left in his structure a weak place through which Providence and all the hosts of authority could stream in and wreck the whole edifice. But contemporary thought was permanently influenced by the boldness of the architecture, which challenged men to compare and contrast it with the servile structure of orthodoxy. In addition to his exaltation of the human reason, Descartes made a contribution to the methods of scientific investigation in the conviction underlying all his work that the laws of nature are invariable. This notion was indispensable to the progress of science. Before it was accepted, no scientist could build on what his predecessors had established. Each had to start from the bare ground, as philosophers have always had to do because their theories cannot be verified by the ordinary tests of experience. They sometimes know that certain foundations would be unsafe, but they can point to none that is certainly safe. But students of natural science have been able, ever since Descartes' time, to start, within certain limitations, from where their predecessors left off.

The progress made in scientific discovery since the close of the seventeenth century has been very rapid. But a price has been paid for this bean-stalk growth and the ever-increasing specialization of the different branches of science; thinkers have had to sacrifice in breadth what they gained in depth. Modern scientists are often accused with justice of being narrow-minded. This accusation does not hold good against seventeenth century thinkers. Theirs was the last age in which a man might take the whole of science for his province.

Professed thinkers were not the only people interested in science. In the seventeenth century, for the first time in the Christian era, scientific knowledge was brought within the reach, not, it is true, of the many, but of the educated. The teaching of Descartes, in spite of the hostility of Jesuit and Jansenist in France, of the obscurantism of the universities in England, was popularized by one of his disciples named Fontenelle (1657–1757), who was a nephew of Corneille. Fontenelle could write in language that was free from technicalities, and as he was interested in all branches of scientific thought, he was able to make known to educated people the progress made over the whole scientific field, and also to show that all branches of knowledge are connected, a contribution to one being a contribution to all. If Descartes had never had such a follower, there is no telling how long the belief in the old geocentric idea of the universe might have prevailed: Descartes himself had not openly denied it, fearing the opposition of ecclesiastical authorities, and Milton seems to have been doubtful about it. But Fontenelle's success made Cartesianism triumphant among the cultured classes of Europe. The Academy of Sciences in Paris and the Royal Society in England, both founded soon after the middle of the seventeenth century, gave a kind of official sanction to scientific research, besides being centres of discussion and experiment. In England, men and women of all sorts caught the infection of the scientific atmosphere; they took to lionizing scientists, would make long expeditions to see the wonders collected by Sir Thomas Browne at Norwich, or would flock to a scientific demonstration with as much zeal as to the newest play. The Duchess of Newcastle, wishing to visit the Royal Society, was, after some debate, duly invited. She was shown "several fine experiments," and was "full of admiration, all admiration." Evelyn and Pepys were both at this meeting, though the attention of the latter was evidently divided between loadstones and microscopes and the "antick" dress of the Duchess. Evelyn's account is more sedate.[1] Charles II would often spend hours of relaxation in his laboratory. In this new-found interest "Cavalier and Roundhead, Churchman and Puritan were for once allied,"[2] and even the poets of the day hastened to pay their homage to the scientific achievement of their age and to celebrate the future fulfilment of its boundless promise. Meanwhile the problems of sanitation were first tackled in a scientific manner, the National Observatory was founded at Greenwich, and Halley made the first Astronomer-Royal. Above all, the greatest genius of the age, Isaac Newton, as yet unknown to fame, was dragging to light the laws that lay behind the seeming chaos into which the universe had fallen with the repudiation of the old and simple cosmology accepted by the Church. What he did for physics, scientists alone can judge, but what he did for the generality of men was to make possible the mechanical triumphs of the nineteenth century which revolutionized the material civilization of the West. Bacon had given mathematics a place below the salt at the banquet

---

[1] *Pepys' Diary, Evelyn's Diary*, May 30, 1667.
[2] Macaulay, *History of England*, 10th edit., 1854, Vol. I, p. 405.

table of the sciences because he thought that mathematical discoveries were of little practical use in increasing the wealth or happiness of men. Could he have foreseen and understood the achievements of the Industrial Revolution and still have retained his utilitarian point of view, he would have given to mathematics pride of place, for all the scientific inventions upon which modern civilization is built depend ultimately upon discoveries made in higher mathematics.

Bacon's utilitarianism is based on a cheerful view of humanity. But it was not until the close of the seventeenth century that the Renaissance finally overcame the pessimism of mediæval thought, which had always been shadowed by the notion of a Fall. The Fall of Rome had closed the Golden Age, and the Age of Innocence had ended with the Fall of Man. If the Renaissance broke the tyranny of Eden, it made fast the shackles of antiquity by exaggerated reverence for Greece and Rome. Again, though the greatest and most creative minds of the Renaissance were humanists of the broadest kind, Machiavelli and Hobbes, anticlerical as they were, had a low opinion of human nature. Above all, the leaders of the Reformation saddled the new churches with a heavier sense of man's natural vice than had ever burdened the Catholics.

The Cartesian revolution in thought finally broke the monopoly of religious pessimism, already threatened by the discoveries of Copernicus. In an age of failure, Pascal's genius would have convinced the world that these discoveries proved the helplessness of man before the might of God: "il écrase l'esprit humain afin de l'anéantir devant Dieu." But by the close of the seventeenth century the people who were interested in Copernicus were also filled with pride by the feats of their age. The universe, they said, is not created specially for man, therefore man must make what he can of the universe. Reason has dispelled the terrors of Hell beneath, it doubts the consolations of Heaven above; it bars the past with its scorn of tradition and superstition, it offers freedom from the conventions and regulations of the present. The true votary of Reason has nothing to depend on but himself; nothing to look to but the future if he is discontented with the present. But Leibniz (1646-1716) taught him not to be discontented with the present because the universe, if not perfect, was as good as it could possibly be.

When the human mind was free at last, and the sovereign state was no longer an ideal but a fact, the work of the Renaissance seemed done. There was, however, one last phase, in which an attempt was made to fuse the two ideals, that is to convert the despotic state to the service of mankind.

CHAPTER V

THE EXPANSION OF THE RENAISSANCE STATES

" Selon la diuersité des humeurs les inclinations sont differentes : & chacun en sa vacation a une fin particulière. Les vns tirēt au proffit, les autres à la gloire, & aucuns au bien public. Le plus grand est au commerce, & principalement celuy qui se faict sur la mer. De là vient le grand soulagement du peuple, l'opulence & l'ornement des republiques." *Les Voyages du Sievr de Champlain . . .*
(1613) ed. the Champlain Society (1922).

" Trade is now become the lady, which in this present age is more courted and celebrated than in any former. . . ."
Quoted Hewins, *English Trade and Finance*, p. 143.

" National power and wealth consist in numbers of people and magazines of home and foreign goods. These depend on trade. . . ."
John Law.
Camb. Mod. Hist., Vol. VI, p. 182.

THE material triumph of Renaissance exploration came in the eighteenth century, when the fitful, eager and spontaneous adventuring energies of the sixteenth century had been driven into the two main channels of trading and colonial development. Just as Frederick the Great and Catharine II tried to man their unpeopled territory and to improve their economic and political resources by internal development and external expansion, so England and France engaged in populating their colonies in America and in developing their trade with all their oversea possessions. And as Sweden and Poland were victimized by Prussia and Russia, so the growing British Empire diminished the colonial empires of France and Holland, while greater Britain itself was halved for a time by the new American nation. It was this expansive energy, partly political, but mainly economic, that produced the greater number of eighteenth century wars. From the economic point of view, colonies were for each country its private store and private clientèle where business did not involve either the transference of gold to possible enemies or the interference of foreigners, who were warned off the premises in a most unhandsome manner, and these economic advantages were valued not only for themselves but also for their contribution to the political consummation of the self-contained national state.

Except for Spain and Portugal, many of whose colonies were planted and to some extent exploited in the age of the Reformation, the sixteenth century was a time of exploration and experiment and the failure of great schemes rather than an epoch of serious colonization. Even Spanish and Portuguese colonization was not inspired, in early days, by the desire to create a new Spain and a new Portugal overseas. The original impulses of all colonization seem to have been impulses of exchange, not of creation. The Portuguese wanted to get wealth in gold and slaves, ivory and silks, spices and jewels; and they wanted scarcely less to give Christianity. In their eastward expansion, trade followed religion as often as religion followed trade: it was Xavier the Jesuit missionary who started the China trade with Portugal. The Spaniards, too, wished to give Christianity and to get gold and silver. Originally they wanted still more to secure the military careers that were being denied to them at home by strong government and the conquest of the Moors. America was won for Spain by a series of astounding military achievements, such as Pizarro's conquest of Peru with 183 men.

Spices and silver, trade and religion, a roving spirit

and national pride were all in the minds of French, English and Dutch adventurers in the sixteenth century. English and Dutch oversea enterprise in Elizabethan days was also a weapon in the struggle with Spain. Raleigh, with the prophetic dream that he vainly laboured to realize in Virginia—the dream of an "England beyond the seas," stood out from the average Elizabethan adventurer. His suggestion that Indians should be brought over from Guiana to be educated in England and to marry English ladies, so that on their return an English-speaking race should grow up with English customs in South America, must have been totally unrepresentative of contemporary opinion.

The Dutch had neither the temperament nor the time to think imperially. Overseas expansion was a matter of life and death to them in the sixteenth century. For when the war of Dutch Independence was at its height, Philip II added Portugal to his empire, and with Portugal came the East Indies. Spain then held the East and West in fee, and threatened to take from the Dutch their trade with the Indies. Rather than lose their main source of livelihood, the Dutch bent their energies to defy Spain and her Portuguese subjects in the Far East as they defied her in Europe. By the close of the seventeenth century they were supreme in the Far East. The seat of their overseas government was in Java. Their possession of Batavia and Malacca gave them the control of the only two known channels of navigation leading from Europe to the coveted Moluccas, those tiny islands freighted with nutmegs and mace and the quarrels of three centuries. Here, by 1630, the Dutch were supreme, having ousted both English and Portuguese. They had driven the Portuguese out of Cochin and had seized the bulk of their trade with China. By the Treaty of Münster (1648), Spain was perpetually excluded from the Eastern trade. In India the trade of the Coromandel coast was in the hands of the Dutch, who also monopolized the cinnamon and pearls of Ceylon. In the East India trade, they were, as Roger Coke complained, "as jealous of a Partner . . . as a Dotard is of a Fair wife, the Pope of his Tripple Crown, or the King of Spain of his West Indies . . ."[1] To the West, they rivalled England and France and Portugal on the coasts of Africa, planted settlements in North America and in the West Indies, while in South America they established a successful colony in Guiana, and for some years ruled over the fairest provinces of Brazil which they had wrested from the Portuguese.

Meanwhile all the other leading nations of Western Europe, France and England, Denmark and Sweden, and even far-away Prussia, began systematically to plant their settlements in East or West. The heyday of experiment and individual enterprise, now stimulated by the encouragement of rulers, now retarded by their indifference or qualms, had passed. Seventeenth century colonization was primarily a governmental activity, which was nevertheless doomed to failure whenever unsupported by public opinion and private capital. The Great Elector's colonial venture for Prussia failed for lack of popular support, and the Danish settlement in India degenerated into a pilfering society for lack of capital.[2]

In England, the interest taken in colonization by the Stuarts culminated in Charles II's time. By the close of the seventeenth century a special department of government, developed from a committee of the Privy Council and known as the Board of Trade and Plantations, was commissioned to look after colonial affairs (1696). Dutch and French colonization bore a still more strongly marked governmental character. In

[1] Roger Coke, *Detection of the Court and State of England*, 1694, Vol. I, p. 420.
[2] *Camb. Mod. Hist.*, IV, 746.

Holland, the two great trading companies who controlled the colonial empire of the Dutch were virtually the state in its commercial aspect. The French colonies were always fostered and ruled directly by the home government.

When colonization had become a recognized part of national life, conquest, exploration and settlement proceeded apace. East and West, the French and English soon rivalled the Dutch, although the Dutch were still the greatest commercial power in the East in 1740. At the opening of the seventeenth century neither England nor France had colonial possessions of importance. At its close they all but divided the eastern rim of North America between them, and they flourished in the West Indies cheek by jowl with the decayed penury of Spanish rule. The French had also established themselves at the mouths of the Mississippi. To the East, both nations maintained successful factories on the coasts of Africa and India, and took an active share in the Slave Trade.

But if at the opening of the eighteenth century France and England held the leading places among colonial powers, their expansion had by no means annihilated the overseas empires of other European states. Holland and Spain still held vast dominions, while Portugal had recovered much of her power with the separation of the Portuguese and Spanish crowns in 1640 and with the expulsion of the Dutch from Brazil fourteen years later.

But the age of discovery was over. Though exploration never ceased entirely, no great results were achieved between the time of Dampier and the time of Cook. Moreover, most of the impulses that had led to the foundation of new colonies were dead. The Bahamas, though discovered, were left unpeopled. In the eighteenth century, colonial powers, like continental powers, expanded either intensively or at the expense of their neighbours. That is one reason why

COLONIAL EXPANSION

colonial development and colonial wars played so great a part in the eighteenth century.

Speaking very broadly there were two main types of colony. The essential difference between the two was this : the one kind existed solely for the sake of Europe, while the other kind developed a life and civilization of its own. On the whole, colonies of the first kind, dead moons of the European system, were older than the colonies with light and life of their own begetting. On the whole, too, colonies of the first kind belonged to the East, and were commercial rather than political; colonies of the second kind belonged to the West and were political rather than commercial. Both were present in Africa and in the West Indies.

Colonization of the first kind meant the planting of small trading stations along the coast of a country. Originally it did not necessarily involve either the conquest of the natives or interference with them : privileges of trade and protection for warehouses and dwellings were the only two essentials. For the factories of Africa and the East did not make or produce things. Everything they wanted, from the pearls of Ceylon to the negroes of Africa, could be obtained either by exchange or by theft. So the men who made the trading colonies did not usually settle there with their families, but came home to Europe when they had made as much money as they could. This was the type of settlement founded by the Portuguese from the late fifteenth century onwards along the coasts of Africa and India, and it was copied with variations all over the East by France, Great Britain and Holland. It explains why India and Africa were known for so long not as continents but as coasts; the Malabar coast and the Coromandel coast; the Ivory, Gold, and Gum coasts. Such stations were necessarily economic rather than political, for they existed only by the permission of the ancient polities they found there. Moreover settlement on a large scale was impossible in the densely peopled East. Above all, for a long time the Europeans could get what they wanted without developing a political life of their own or interfering with that of the native states. Their first and chief concern was with the wares of the East and their own profits.

The second or "political" type of colony usually grew up later and belonged to the West rather than to the East. In America, political life was possible because there was room for it. America, no less than India, had its different races and its various civilizations; but as compared with the East, the West was empty of men and of institutions. There, too, political life was not only possible, but necessary to European enterprise. The West offered no trade in manufactured goods. Its typical natural products were first cultivated on a large scale by Europeans. There was virtually no trading with the natives for silver or gold, nor for slaves, though in the north the fur trade was important. On the whole, whatever Europeans wanted they had to get for themselves. Mining and agriculture, and to a less extent fur-hunting and lumbering, involved more permanent settlement and a wider territorial basis than did the mere exchange of goods that characterized European dealings with the Far East. Where men settle permanently with their wives and children they form a society, that is a group capable of political life. It must be remembered, however, that external politics were more important in the trading-stations of the East than in the colonies of the West. The political relations of Indians and Europeans had comparatively little influence on the life and history of the American colonies: in the East, on the contrary, European settlements owed their existence and much of their prosperity to the political and commercial treaties they contracted with native powers.

The difference between the two types of settlement, never so wide before the nineteenth century as that which separates a country exploited by "peaceful penetration" from a country governed by "Dominion Home Rule," was great enough to make it natural for colonial powers to act towards their settlements sometimes as sovereigns, sometimes as merchants. It was natural, if not wise, to regard the factories of India as mere commercial propositions; it was neither natural nor wise so to regard the aristocratic society of Virginia. But the mother-countries usually chose their rôle not in regard to the nature of the colony but in the service of their own interests and ideals. To the French, whose greatness rested primarily on political and military organization, political interests were always paramount in the colonial sphere; while the Dutch, who lived by trade and shipping, regarded their colonies almost exclusively from a commercial point of view. If the French and Spanish were always sovereigns and the Dutch always merchants, the English were sometimes one and sometimes the other.

It was natural that governments should think of colonies as private property, because all settlements had originally been made in the name of some European crown and were admittedly royal possessions in which the land, products and trade could be granted or sold at the pleasure and price of the ruler.

From this common origin sprang political groups of an infinite variety. In the commercial settlements of the East, government, such as it was, consisted usually of regulations made by chartered companies. This, however, was not the case with the Portuguese settlements, where, in the absence of chartered companies,[1] government was organized on the more elaborate plan originally adopted in the colonies of Venice. But among the colonies of the West, political differences were almost as marked as those which

[1] Until late in the eighteenth century.

separated them as a whole from the "factories" of the East.

Spanish colonization was primarily the outcome of two fundamental race-characteristics, militancy and religious fervour. The soldier and the Jesuit were the natural rulers of the Spanish colony, and the natural enemies of independent political life. The climate was on their side. Spanish pride completed their victory. At first none but Castilians, later none but orthodox Spaniards, had the right to enter the colonies. Spanish customs, Spanish social distinctions and disdain of manual labour were all faithfully reproduced there. Men who settled permanently were looked down upon, and their children were stigmatized as "creoles," while Spaniards, born in Spain, carried on the important work of government and made what money they could out of it, only to regard Spain as their real home. The trade of the colonies, such as it was, passed from royal control into the hands of a few Seville merchants.[1] The natural result was that Spanish America had for hundreds of years scarcely any independent life of its own.

French colonization was a characteristic expression of Louis XIV's highly concentrated Renaissance State, resting on military and administrative efficiency, intent upon widening its sway. Though the French government had certain concrete ends in view such as the discovery of gold, the sovereign purpose and the main effect of French exploration and missionary enterprise, of French persistence in trying to understand and to educate native peoples was to add new provinces to France. French feudal law and French religion prevailed: heretics were excluded.[2] But unlike the

---

[1] There was a considerable relaxation of this system in the last quarter of the eighteenth century.

[2] This was not the case, however, in the French West Indies where Colbert allowed the immigration of Jews and Protestants in order to increase the small number of white people. *Camb. Mod. Hist.*, VII, p. 86.

Spaniards, the French were not racially exclusive. Every means was used to increase the size of the colonial population. Not only permanent settlers and their descendants, but even the children of mixed French and Indian blood were accounted sons of France. Intermarriage with Indians was actively encouraged. But everything was thought out and promoted by the home government. In France there was no special board to deal with colonial affairs, which were included in the work of the Minister of the Marine. The religious and military needs of Canada were supplied by France; Canadian taxation was imposed by France; Canadian trade was in the hands of a company created by the French government. The Governors of Canada were assisted by Intendants who held in New France the same position that they held at home. And as in Spanish America, the national tendency in colonial development was strengthened by natural conditions. The harsh climate and poor soil of Eastern Canada helped to limit both the numbers and wealth of the French population and so to rivet the chain of their dependence on the mother-country. In the West Indies, richest and most prosperous of French overseas dominions, military necessity, in the shape of English, Dutch and Spanish rivalry at uncomfortably close quarters, must have cemented the close bonds between colonies and the mother-country even if the connection had been less economically advantageous than it actually was.

If the French government of Louis XIV's successors had maintained its seventeenth century efficiency it might have prevented the colonial triumph of England. From a military point of view the French colonies had the superior position; if the Family Compact could be made effective it was not too much to hope that the Franco-Spanish fleets might break the naval supremacy of England. Above all, the French had a vigorous and comprehensive colonial policy in working order.

The defence of the West Indies, for instance, was not an emergency measure to be enterprised at the eleventh hour; it was an essential function of the ordinary colonial administration carried out by the mother-country. The settlers in the English islands complained bitterly of the lack of equal solicitude on the part of their home government. This was typical of the contrast between the colonial government of France and England. But in the eighteenth century the numerical superiority of the English in America told as heavily in their favour against the French as it had formerly done against the Dutch, and it was probably this more than any other single advantage which ensured the success of Great Britain.

The English colonies in America were of a more independent type. The policy of the mother-country until the second half of the seventeenth century helped the colonies to develop on their own lines. Foreign settlers were admitted, religious freedom was tacitly allowed, and on the whole commercial regulations were generous and political control was not unduly pressed. The most vigorous of the colonies were not indeed so much an extension of the home government as an expression of variance with it. They were founded not with the vague general aim of increasing the glory of England but with a definite particular object such as freedom to worship in the Puritan or Quaker or Roman Catholic fashion. In the English colonies of the West there were three main kinds of government, crown government, proprietary government and charter government. The charter colonies of New England had a great measure of independence. They elected their own governors and taxed and defended themselves. Massachusetts once went to war with France on its own initiative and formed a confederation with its neighbour states without asking for the permission of Great Britain. The proprietary colonies, too, were free from direct depen-

COLONIAL EXPANSION

dence on the British executive. Their charters, no less than those of the New England colonies, allowed a wide measure of free political development because local constitution-making was subject merely to the general proviso that the laws and procedure adopted should be as conformable as possible to the English models. Even crown government allowed in practice a measure of local initiative. While Virginia was still governed by a company, a house of burgesses "broke out." This democratic distemper, by no means contemplated in the company's charter, was not doctored by the crown when royal control superseded company company government in 1624.

Thus the customs and laws of England were reproduced in her colonies, but the closeness of the copy was decided by the colonists rather than by the home government. The climate of the northern colonies was some guarantee for their independent spirit. Neither so hot as to be enervating nor too cold to be invigorating, it encouraged industry and did not discourage immigration. Too much stress must not, however, be laid on the influence of climate, because even the West Indian colonies, with their tropical heat and consequent reliance upon a negro population which greatly outnumbered the colonists, were for centuries[1] extremely tenacious of their political privileges.

French and Spanish colonies certainly had a life of their own, just as Normandy or Castile had. But the French colonies had little more than a provincial life, while the Spanish colonies had somewhat less. But the English colonies in North America, in spite of their long-continued connection with the mother-country, were creating national lives of their own with which the provincial life of Yorkshire, for instance, could not bear comparison.

[1] Jamaica finally gave up her democratic form of government because it gave too great political power to the negroes.

Very different from the English colonies were the Dutch settlements, which nevertheless offer a still greater contrast to those of the French. The French tried to import their essentially political and military conception of colonization into their Indian "factories": the Dutch tried to govern their Western colonies by the mercantile principles of their rule in the Far East. Quebec is the apple of a soldier's eye: New York the answer to a merchant's prayer.

The New Netherlands existed for the fur-trade. Its land-owners were absentees; its settlers were allowed neither freedom of development nor adequate defence. Its very frontiers were left undefined. Consequently the colony had no political life, and less than forty years after its foundation it passed quietly under English control. The Dutch settlement at the Cape of Good Hope was originally a port of call for the East Indiamen. Later it was found that the soil further inland was peculiarly suited to cattle raising and sheep farming, with the result that a considerable number of Dutch settlers, reinforced by French Huguenots and Germans, created a peculiar society of their own, primitive no doubt, but with all the elements of political and social development. Their sovereign was the Dutch East India Company which understood little and cared less about the rights and interests of the people under its rule. Ungenerous in granting freehold, it allowed the settlers to have no political privileges whatever and restricted their economic freedom in every possible way. For instance, they might not communicate with the ships of other countries; they might not even sail themselves to bordering shores to get the fuel they needed. When after various vicissitudes in the Napoleonic Wars they passed finally to Great Britain, they do not seem to have resented the change of masters.

But in spite of the differences separating French and Dutch colonies they were alike in being extensions of

COLONIAL EXPANSION

their home governments. Just as Canadian institutions were as faithful an expression as circumstances allowed of the political institutions and ideals of France, so was each Dutch settlement virtually an extension of the Dutch government. For the two great companies which ruled the colonial empire of Holland were literally the Dutch state in its economic aspect, since Dutch towns had their delegates in the companies just as they sent delegates to the States-General. The Governor-General in Java, the headquarters of the Dutch Eastern Empire, was nominated for a period of five years only by the East India Company at home which exercised as complete a control as possible over colonial affairs.

It was partly owing to the great differences between the English colonies, and partly to dynastic changes, but still more to the opportunist conception which the mother-country had formed of the political uses of overseas dominions, that the relations between England and her colonies were not nearly so close nor so clearly defined as the relations existing between other countries and their dependencies. England and France were agreed that colonies were an encouragement to shipping and so to sea-power, that they were useful pawns in the game of European politics and useful "dumping-grounds" for undesirables; they agreed with Holland that they had economic uses. But England, who also saw, however indistinctly, a safety-valve for dissent in her colonies, regarded all these uses as ends in themselves. In the long run, her hand-to-mouth policy recoiled on her in the complete lack of sympathetic vision and purpose which most of her eighteenth century ministers displayed in dealing with colonial questions, but in the seventeenth century it enabled her to abstain as a general rule from meddling over much in the local politics of her dependencies.

But if to England and Spain colonies were contributions to the national life, to Holland they were the chief means of a livelihood, while to France they were integral elements of a civilization. Holland could not afford to relax control over details of colonial life and administration any more than a successful manufacturer can afford to neglect the details of management in his business. France adopted a similar policy from a different point of view. Unlike all the other colonizing powers, who were still in the stage of giving and taking—mostly the latter—France was consciously creative. She was therefore under the necessity of handling her material herself. Other nations wanted colonies and took them when they could, assessing them at their individual worth and face-value. France, though by no means blind to this aspect of colonization, valued her possessions above all for their collective and potential use; to her they were more than precious stones to be counted singly, because they were also contributory elements to a dazzling whole. Each was a separate jewel in the stupendous diadem of imperial destiny.

If national differences had thus led the mother-countries to form different conceptions of colonial sovereignty, the growing belief in the mercantile system gave a certain unity to the economic side of the colonial policy which they followed for about a century before the French Revolution. Not that it is possible to divorce their economic from their political sovereignty. We saw earlier how the mercantile system was political as well as economic—how at its root was the desire for the national power, but how the idea that the basis of power might be economic as much as if not more than political was steadily gaining ground. Consequently colonies came to be regarded not so much as political dominions but as economic assets. It was this growing belief in the commercial basis of power that inclined countries, irrespective of their own national bent, to treat all their settlements, whether Eastern or Western, on commercial lines, to act as exploiters rather than parents, as merchants rather than sovereigns.

From an economic point of view colonies were valued for three main reasons; first for their commodities; secondly for the growth of foreign trade which the possession of those commodities would stimulate, and thirdly for the encouragement of the various trades[1] and industries of the mother-country. England and France valued their colonies from all three points of view; Portugal and Holland chiefly from the second point of view, while Spain valued hers almost exclusively from the first point of view. Spain neither developed her colonies extensively so as to make herself economically independent of other powers, nor encouraged her industries at home to supply colonial needs. On the contrary, having acquired an enormous increase of capital she sat down to live on it. Her energies were absorbed in the fruitless task of preventing other people from sharing it.

Other nations did not live on their capital, but they were quite as anxious as Spain to preserve their colonial monopolies.

Assuming the possibility and desirability of enclosing and fattening the trade of each nation behind impregnable tariff bars, there were still two policies open to colonial powers. They might consider mother-country and colonies as equal members of one great self-sufficient state and reserve their differential treatment for foreign nations. If England had adopted this policy she could still have made herself economically independent of the Continent; she could have anticipated the imperialism of the late nineteenth century. The second policy was to differentiate against both colony and foreign nations in favour of the mother-country alone.

---

[1] From a mercantilist point of view colonial trade had the advantage over foreign trade, because it did not take precious metals into foreign, possibly enemy, countries.

That the imperial possibility was thought of, we know. Individuals advocated it, governments, both French and English, sometimes tried to realize it. But the commercial actuality was the child of government necessity and of trading interests. Having neither the capital nor the organization necessary for colonization, governments were forced to convert an imperial advantage, nominally enjoyed by the crown, into the national or sectional monopoly of a company. Again, governments might wish to encourage colonial development, and were able to do so as long as the business interests at home did not materially suffer thereby. But in Holland the trading classes were supreme, in England their influence was great and increasing, while even in France, where they had little political power, their importance was clearly realized, and their interests consulted.

The colonial interests of the trading classes are bitingly described by Adam Smith in his famous description of the relations between England and her colonies in the eighteenth century. " The cultivators " [*i.e.* the American colonists], he says, " . . became in the course of a little more than thirty or forty years (between 1620 and 1660) so numerous and thriving a people that the shopkeepers and other traders of England wished to secure to themselves the monopoly of their custom . . . they petitioned the parliament that the cultivators of America might for the future be confined to their shop ; first, for buying all the goods which they wanted from Europe ; and, secondly, for selling all such parts of their own produce as those traders might find it convenient to buy."[1]

At the same time it is clear that the interests of the trading classes often coincided with the supposed interests of the state. National self-sufficiency, the first political principle of mercantilism, no less than the prosperity of manufacturers, rested on a cheap and

[1] *Wealth of Nations* (Everyman's Lib. Edit.), Vol. II, p. 111.

COLONIAL EXPANSION 125

plentiful supply of raw materials and on the discouragement of colonial manufactures. For if the colonies were allowed to export whither they pleased, not only would the supply of raw materials to the mother-country be diminished and her dependence on other states increased, but her potential enemies would be helped. Again, if the colonies found manufactures profitable, much of their energy would be turned aside from producing raw material. Thus reasons of state as well as the influence of the commercial classes impelled governments to combine the rôles of merchant and sovereign.

One result of this necessity was the double nature of the methods by which countries tried to keep their double colonial monopoly. The Cromwellian Navigation Act, for instance, appears as an attempt to protect and to foster the shipping industries, but its primary object was to break the Dutch monopoly of the carrying trade. Again, the trade restriction imposed on the colonists by the Caroline Navigation Act was meant not only to help British industries but also to make England economically independent of the Continent. Conversely, the chartered companies which controlled the bulk of colonial trade all the world over were allowed perforce to strengthen their commercial monopoly with many a political attribute of sovereignty. The Dutch East India Company appointed magistrates and administered justice; it appointed generals and governors and made peace and war; it levied troops and it coined money. In 1625 the Royal Proclamation of Charles I had disparaged the political pretensions of companies "To whom it may be proper to trust matters of trade, but cannot be fit or safe to commit the ordering of state affairs be they never of so mean a consequence."[1] But colonization would have stopped had the English government

[1] Egerton, *A Short History of British Colonial Policy*, 2nd ed., 1905, p. 44.

lived up to its haughty principle. France, it is true, did not devolve so many regalian rights on her companies as the English and Dutch did, but it is significant that the French companies, whether for this reason or not, were one of the most unsuccessful agents of French colonization. The French West Indies prospered best after the dissolution of the trading companies.

In their treatment of natives, again, European governments faced two ways owing to their acting now as merchants, now as sovereigns. At first sight it is strange to find that the constitutional states of England and Holland felt little responsibility for the treatment of native races while the autocratic governments of France and Spain at least endeavoured by wise and careful laws to safeguard the lives and interests both of negroes and of Indians. Indeed, negro slavery was first started in Spanish America as a humanitarian experiment to save the Indians from work for which their physique did not fit them. A closer examination seems to show that the more commercial its colonial policy, the more inhuman the colonizing power. Raleigh, the first English imperialist, had advocated kind treatment of natives and had put his principles into practice as far as he could. The imperialism of Louis XIV dictated not only the Revocation of the Edict of Nantes, but also the *Code Noir* which gave important rights and some privileges to the negroes. The Spanish government, autocratic, tyrannical and exclusive, took more pains than perhaps any other to secure fair treatment for the native races under its rule. But the Dutch and English, though on the whole tolerant of native beliefs and customs, treated native peoples rather as animals than as men, making with certain exceptions no real attempt to understand them or to conciliate them such as the French made both in Canada and in India. Only when the English were forced to fight the French with their own weapons did they try to follow suit in order to gain allies among the Indians of East and West.

That the governmental intentions of France and Spain were not carried out where mining and plantation interests were strong merely goes to show further that in the seventeenth and eighteenth centuries, as too often now, commercial policy favours exploitation of native races while a true governmental policy favours their protection. As Adam Smith said of the companies in India, "their mercantile habits draw them . . . almost necessarily, though perhaps insensibly, to prefer upon all ordinary occasions the little and transitory profit of the monopolist to the great and permanent revenue of the sovereign. . . . As sovereigns their interest is exactly the same with that of the country which they govern. As merchants their interest is directly opposite to that interest."[1]

Whether national and other differences stressed the mercantile or the imperial side of colonial policy, all European governments were, then, both merchants and sovereigns to their colonies. They saw in the possession of colonies a means of strengthening the life of their state, now on the political, now on the economic side. This was what they fought for with the quasi-economic and peaceful means of exclusive companies, navigation acts, commercial treaties, tariff regulations and " prevention " men. But in the last resort was the supreme political measure of war.

[1] *Wealth of Nations*, Vol. II, p. 134.

CHAPTER VI

THE AGE OF REASON

" . . . Si l'on bannit l'homme ou l'être pensant & contemplateur de dessus la surface de la terre ; ce spectacle pathétique & sublime de la nature n'est plus qu'une scène triste et muette. L'univers se taît ; le silence & la nuit s'en emparent."

Diderot, *Encyclopédie* (Art. " *Encyclopédie* "), Vol. V (Paris, 1754).

" The nature of man is far from being in itself evil ; it abounds with benevolence, charity, and pity, coveting praise and honour and shunning shame and disgrace. Bad education, bad habits, and bad customs debauch our nature, and drive it headlong as it were into vice. The governors of the world, and I am afraid the priesthood, are answerable for the badness of it."

Fielding, *Amelia*, Bk. IX, ch. v.

" The age of chivalry is gone. That of sophisters, economists and calculators, has succeeded ; and the glory of Europe is extinguished for ever."

Burke, *Reflections on the French Revolution*.

' . . . et l'empire de la terre ne vaut pas un bon estomac."

Voltaire, *Lettre à M. de Cideville*, 1757.

IN the eighteenth century people prided themselves on being practical and orderly. They tried to domesticate the soaring ideas of the Renaissance, to label them and to put them to practical uses. The men of thought turned their attention from cosmic to human problems ; the men of action translated humanitarianism into new hospitals, prison reform and more lenient penal codes. Together they effected the betrothal of science and industry. They reasoned religion into a polite convention. They arranged and classified their heritage of knowledge by producing encyclopædias, writing great histories, founding museums and universities, codifying laws, inventing systems of botanical and zoological classification. The whole process was the counterpart of the crystallization that forms of government and society had slowly undergone.

Renaissance thinkers and writers had lived in an age of unsettlement and wonder. The old landmarks of church and empire, manor and walled town were being obliterated. New countries, new peoples, new religions, a new order of society flashed into view. None could predict the future : none could recapture the immediate past. But by the latter part of the seventeenth century, civilization had stayed its giddy whirl. The political problem had been solved by the despotic state. Religious controversies had for the most part sunk their fires in the ashes of indifference. Undiscovered countries almost ceased to attract the adventurous : colonization was now a policy, not an inspiration. The Age of Reason was a season of stock-taking rather than of new ventures.

As might be expected, the most influential philosophy of such an age was neither profound nor strikingly original. Whether it sprang from the well-known English school of Locke, "the intellectual ruler of the eighteenth century,"[1] or from French writers of less fame, its headquarters were in France and its propaganda influenced the greater part of Europe. Its most marked feature was this—man was its goal and starting-point, humanity its sole standard of worth.

From a humanitarian point of view, the work of the Renaissance could be continued and improved in two ways. In the first place it could be broadened. Intellectual freedom might be won for the many instead of for the few, and as a necessary corollary to

[1] Leslie Stephen, *English Thought in the Eighteenth Century*, Vol. I, p. 86.

this, the advance made in the abstract fields of philosophy and science might be paralleled in the more concrete spheres of administration and material comfort. In the second place the double work of the Renaissance might be unified into a resplendent whole. For hitherto, the paramount creations of the Renaissance, the sovereign state and the independent man, had not only developed on separate lines, but had clearly warred against each other. The state of Louis XIV was in many ways inhuman: the pretensions of Calvin did not square with state sovereignty. But once the state was humanized, despotism and humanity would each serve the other. So only one more stage had to be passed before the golden age was won.

This was not the idle dream of an ecstatic visionary: it was the considered opinion of the most influential men of the most clear-thinking country in the world, and they lived in that half-century of history which is distinguished above all others for common sense.

These French philosophers of the eighteenth century were the last heirs of the Renaissance in direct line of descent. D'Alembert recognized the spiritual forbears of himself and his friends. He held that the "philosophic" movement of his own day was the third and best stage of that civilization which had begun with "la Renaissance des lettres." Except for Greece and Rome all that lay behind was "la barbarie." In his long introduction to the *Encyclopædia*, that great attempt to make a summary of human knowledge, he inserted short appreciations of the great Renaissance figures such as Bacon and Descartes in token that his work rested upon theirs. Early in the following century De Maistre tried to confute Bacon because he believed that the ungodly philosophy of the eighteenth century was entirely due to his influence. D'Alembert and his friends are chiefly famous because they wiped the inhuman creed of Louis XIV from the tablets of French approval and left them bare for the holy writ of revolution. For this they are truly called heralds of a new age. But first and foremost they were champions of the old.

The French philosophers could not accept unqualified the optimism of Leibniz. Perhaps there were actually more people in the eighteenth century who were completely satisfied with life than there have been in any other age, but they belonged to the ruling and leisured classes. When the *Philosophes* looked further afield they saw that to all appearance the world was not good. La Bruyère's description of the French peasants as "certains animaux farouches" who when they rise from bending over their toil show " une face humaine " was no doubt coloured by his sardonic humour, but the fact that such a description could be written at all in the golden age of France gives an unpleasant hint of what social conditions must have been in more backward countries.

On the whole it seems fair to say that the eighteenth century had retained most of the abuses of the mediæval ecclesiastical and social system, and none of its virtues. Priests could still persecute the body and mind and they no longer gave spiritual and mental food. Lords still exacted feudal dues and no longer gave protection and justice. Gilds still multiplied their regulations, though they no longer encouraged trade but stifled it. Everywhere it was the same: those in authority did nothing useful in return for the power they held. No wonder Candide mistrusted Leibniz and his optimism. " Qu'est-ce qu' optimisme ? " asked Cacambo, his servant. "'Hélas,' dit Candide, ' c'est la rage de soutenir que tout est bien quand on est mal.' "[1]

It was the contrast between the wretched condition of the many and the enlightened luxury of the few that drove eighteenth century thinkers, especially in France, to apply reason to the problems of social and

[1] Voltaire, *Candide*, p. 134, ed. Nilsson.

political reform. By so doing they hoped to make true for all the faith of the fortunate,—faith in the goodness and sufficiency of human life on earth. It was surely arguable that the successes won by reason in the field of abstract thought could be paralleled in the sphere of the concrete. And as the " philosophy " of the Voltairean school was thus a programme of practical reform and not simply a system of abstract theory, it was shaped more by the actual social, political and ecclesiastical problems of the time than by the thought of its forerunners.

The French philosophers differed too greatly in their opinions to be called a school. Voltaire, de St. Pierre and Montesquieu believed in God; Helvétius, d'Holbach and Diderot were atheists. But it is possible to form a general idea of the groundwork of their teaching. Their humanitarianism was broad but not exalted. Humanity included not only the living but the unborn. At best man was born good, at worst he could be made good. All men were naturally equal, whether rich or poor, black or white, pagan or Christian, German or Japanese; though when it came to Frenchmen and Jews the *Philosophes* could not overcome their prejudice in favour of the one and against the other. From the contrast between the natural innocence of man and his actual misery they drew two conclusions. Either a better time must be coming— they must be at the dawn of civilization, not at its height, or man's nature must have been warped by something unnatural. For the most part they held these two alternatives together, some of them leaning more upon the one, some upon the other: that is, they believed in the indefinite perfectibility of man whose natural destiny of happiness and good was being frustrated by artificial restraints.

It sometimes seems as if the *Philosophes* worshipped a co-equal trinity of reason, nature and humanity, but more probably their appeal to reason and nature was instrumental to their single god, humanity. They did no more than accept a debased and popularized form of seventeenth century philosophy—they neither developed nor defined the ideas of reason and nature, but simply took them, second-hand and badly worn, as useful vehicles for their thought. People who oppose Proportional Representation to-day would not be listened to if they based their arguments solely on the absence of the system in the Ark; they must bring forward facts that look scientific. So, after the Cartesian revolution in thought, it was both easier and more effectual for Voltaire and d'Alembert to condemn a doctrine or an institution because it was "unreasonable" or "unnatural" than because it was merely "inhuman." Just as we have a slipshod idea of the theory of evolution, and often use it almost unconsciously as the framework of our thought, so the *Philosophes* of the eighteenth century used their popular and ill-defined conceptions of reason and nature as the normal medium of expression.

To Descartes reason seems to have meant an almost superhuman faculty the fragmentary possession of which gives us kinship with God and knowledge of truth: to us it perhaps means most generally the free exercise of individual criticism in thought and conduct. But to the *Philosophe* it meant the use of common sense. Common sense must approve anything useful to man, and condemn everything harmful or useless to him. De St. Pierre believed in heaven and hell because he thought them useful. Voltaire believed in immortality—or said he did—for the same reason. He maintained that if God did not exist, that is if reason had definitely disproved His existence, it would be necessary to invent Him because belief in God was helpful to humanity. Again and again he poured ridicule and contempt upon the criminal idiocy of war, the third and worst scourge of mankind. Pest and famine we owed to Providence, but war was our own invention. " C'est sans doute un très bel art que celui qui désole les campagnes, détruit les habitations et fait périr, année commune, quarante mille hommes sur cent mille." A prince claims on flimsy genealogical grounds that a province belongs to him by "divine right." He collects a number of men who have nothing to do and nothing to lose, " les fait tourner à droite et à gauche, et marche à la gloire." Other princes prick up their ears and cover the land with more "meurtriers mercénaires." The opposing hosts have no notion why they are fighting each other ; the only thing all are agreed on is to do as much harm as possible. Each side calls on God most solemnly before going to exterminate the other. He gets no thanks if two or three thousand are killed, but when the slaughter rises to ten thousand, and the destruction of a town is thrown in, a lengthy song of praise will reward him. Meanwhile the preachers who all the rest of the year have busily described the eternal punishment in store for the ladies who use rouge or for the poor man who eats a bit of mutton in Lent, now celebrate the orgy of murder, and tell us what was done long ago in Palestine " à propos d'un combat en Vétéravie." Yet "tous les vices réunis de tous les âges et de tous les lieux n' egaleront jamais les maux que produit une seule campagne."[1] D'Alembert and that incorrigible optimist the Abbé de St. Pierre expressed the same point of view when they decried the worship paid to famous conquerors and would have raised altars to scientists instead, to unknown technical inventors, wheelwrights and smiths, and the builders of roads and bridges. The soldiers destroyed life and the others enlarged it. But "les noms de ces bienfaiteurs du genre humain sont presque tous inconnus, tandis que l'histoire de ses destructeurs, c'est à dire des conquérans, n'est ignorée de personne."[2] Could anything be more unreasonable ?

[1] Voltaire, *Dictionnaire Philosophique*, article "*Guerre.*"
[2] D'Alembert, *Discours Préliminaire de l'Encyclopédie. Œuvres.* Vol. I, p. 54 (Paris, 1821).

By Nature seventeenth century thinkers probably meant, to put it very roughly, the universe as revealed not by faith, but by reason. God's existence might be inferred from natural phenomena, but not proved by miracles or revelation. As Voltaire put it, " . . . qui fait un ouvrage, sinon un ouvrier ? Qui fait des lois, sinon un législateur ? Il y a donc un ouvrier, un législateur éternel."[1] But because reason meant common sense to the eighteenth century *Philosophes* they had a more materialistic idea of nature than many of the seventeenth century thinkers. On the other hand they seem to have confounded the seventeenth century view with a Rabelaisian conception of " natural " as opposed to " artificial."

But just as the philosophic movement was practical rather than theoretical, so on the whole the Voltairean conception of reason and nature was shaped not so much by deliberate and unbiased thought as by hostility to definite institutions and vices which seemed pre-eminently inhuman. Many of the social and political evils of the time were clearly due to inequality of opportunity. Therefore according to nature and reason, the artificial barriers of society and industry—" cette fastidieuse uniformité "—ought to be scrapped : all men ought to have equal chances. The worst intellectual evils of the time, superstition, ignorance and fear, were due to the tyranny of an unseen world. Therefore according to nature and reason, either there is no unseen world or else it has no direct influence upon earth. God created this world, and then withdrew to the clouds. Perhaps he looked on : certainly he did not interfere. The most glaring moral abuses were due chiefly to cruelty and hypocrisy. Therefore the only two unforgivable sins, those against nature and reason, are cruelty and hypocrisy ; and the paramount virtues, those that

---

[1] *Dict. Phil.*, p. 67.

ennoble the natural and reasonable man, are kindness and toleration and intellectual honesty.[1]

There is little or no philosophy in this. It is an attempt to find out, not what is real, but what is useful for the particular purposes of mankind, given the particular data of man's natural goodness and of his complete responsiveness to environment. It is philanthropy in the broadest though not in the deepest sense of the word, for whatever the *Philosophes* were, and they were many things at once, they were seldom candidates for prison, never for the stake.[2] On the intellectual side they were indulgent grandmothers to mankind, insisting that the virtues of man were due to natural sweetness of disposition, and that the parental restraints imposed by governments and churches were responsible for all his misdemeanours. On the political side they corresponded to moderate liberals, for they aimed to compass human happiness by altering man's environment through legislation and education, not by violent economic or political revolution. And on the social side they were for the most part cultivated gentlemen of the world with a wide range of interests and a very pretty wit.

What the *Philosophes* hoped to do depended partly on their temperaments, partly on their ages. Few had the optimism of de St. Pierre. For him hope was as good as certainty. He had wonderful " projets " for every evil under the sun, from the disputes of theologians to the badness of roads in winter. For Voltaire the millennium receded as age advanced, though he never lost sight of it. Again, there were two generations of *Philosophes*. The first generation, of which Montesquieu was the most famous member, was conservative, aristocratic and chiefly interested

[1] Compare Fielding's hero Tom Jones whose many failings scarcely seem to count against him because he is never hypocritical and never cruel.

[2] Grimm said that the most enlightened reasoning in the world was not worth a night in the Bastille.

in constitutional abuses. Of other unreasonable evils they exposed the nature and folly but did not attempt their practical reform. The second generation, including d'Alembert, Helvétius, Diderot and Rousseau, were less conservative, less aristocratic and less interested in constitutional questions. Between them they claimed the whole of human knowledge for their province; as practical reformers they were most interested in social and ecclesiastical problems. Voltaire (1694-1778), who was born before Racine's death, belonged originally to the earlier generation, but late in life he transferred his activities to the younger group. Old, and constantly at death's door, he was the most indefatigable worker of them all, and will always stand as the most brilliant representative of the whole movement.

Montesquieu (1689-1755) was in a sense the pioneer of this last phase of the Renaissance. His greatest achievement was to apply the method of Descartes to social phenomena. Before his day it had been usual to hold that the prosperity or misery of different peoples at different times was due to the will of God Who had ordained the course of history for His own mysterious purpose. Montesquieu refused to believe this. For years on end he collected facts about different periods and countries, and hoped to induce from them the general laws to which political events, he supposed, must be subject. If he could do this he would be able not only to point out, but to remedy, the causes of the decline and fall of empires.

As a political philosopher his aim was to humanize the state; to make it reasonable. If governments want to increase the number of their subjects they must act mildly because liberty attracts strangers. Monarchy ought to be the best form of government, but in fact it is often bad. Despotism ought therefore to be tempered by some other principle, preferably that of aristocracy. But as experience has shown, forms of government must depend upon all kinds of circumstances, geographical, racial and climatic : there is therefore no ideal form of government. To impose an aristocracy upon Great Britain would be to destroy the state, because the history and character of the English had fitted them for a different polity.

Religion he looked at from a far more scientific and detached point of view than either Voltaire or d'Holbach who were so much impressed by its abuses that they had no eyes for anything else. To Montesquieu religion was simply one of the many causes that make or mar a nation: in *De l'Esprit des Lois* he places it between population and police. He thought of God as sitting in detached majesty above the clouds,—too high, one infers, to trouble about men, too remote for them to trouble about him.

But though both his method and ideas came from the Renaissance, and make it natural to connect him with the main group of eighteenth century thinkers in France, Montesqiueu had some ideas which were foreign to the Renaissance and the Voltaireans. Though an experimental scientist in the early part of his life and always anxious to think scientifically, he was perhaps the only influential writer of the Renaissance tradition to see that the growth of scientific knowledge might bring curses to mankind as well as blessings. As a political thinker he was alone in wanting to limit the power of monarchy. D'Argenson wanted to decentralize the government of France, but to increase the royal power at the same time. De St. Pierre, who thought that political reform would waft man from the age of silver to the age of gold, wanted France to be governed by councils, but these councils were to divide the power not of the king but of the "premier ministre."

Again, in stressing the influence upon human destinies of uncontrollable forces such as climate, Montesquieu implied that men were unable to mould their own lives. This fatalism was anathema to Helvétius and Voltaire who believed in the unconditioned power of man-made laws. It is true that Montesquieu appears also to have held a doctrine more like theirs, for he sometimes writes as if he thought that wisely-chosen laws could bring prosperity. Whether they saw this contradiction or not, neither Helvétius nor Voltaire had a high opinion of *De l'Esprit des Lois*.

The work of the second generation of *Philosophes* was more practical though less constructive than the work of Montesquieu or of de St. Pierre. Instead of inventing constitutions and diagnosing political diseases, the first aims of Voltaire and his younger contemporaries were to divorce religion from its inhuman partner the Church, and to abolish all unreasonable laws, whether in society, industry or courts of justice; whether against freedom of thought, writing or speech.

But they had a conservative aim too. Unlike Montesquieu and d'Argenson, Voltaire and Diderot approved of unqualified autocracy as long as it was humane. None of them were democrats. Their humanity, like everything else in the eighteenth century, lacked reverence. It was a condescending virtue which never accorded the average man a status higher than that of a good child, though never lower than that of a teachable monkey. Montesquieu thought that men were " fripons en détails et en gros honnêtes hommes." Such creatures cannot govern. Indeed, Voltaire's ideal polity was more like a glorified " Royal Society for the Prevention of Cruelty to Animals " than like a modern " democratic " state.

Thirdly, the Voltaireans had a constructive aim. Human monkeys and even good children must be educated to see the folly of intolerance, war and asceticism, and the common sense of living at peace with one's neighbours and of keeping out of the doctor's clutches. Ignorance, as Erasmus had taught, was the arch-enemy of mankind.

Education was not only an aim but a weapon. The *Philosophes* undertook the overwhelming task of educating France. If they educated France they would go far to educate Europe. To do this they both used and circumvented existing institutions in France. They ridiculed petticoat government, but hid behind its skirts; they exposed the Jesuits, but made use of their teaching; they avoided the censorship by criticizing French government under another name, and orthodoxy under the name of heresy, or by publishing their books in London, Amsterdam and Geneva. They not only wrote books by the score, but with the exception of de St. Pierre, books that people would read. Montesquieu's style is like Montaigne's—the "badinage d'un grand penseur." He and Voltaire and Diderot were amusing, epigrammatic, witty and caustic: Voltaire at least was never monotonous and never long-winded. Letters they wrote by the hundred. Ten thousand of Voltaire's survive, and they are addressed to seven hundred different people. Most important of all, they talked. This had more effect in the eighteenth century than it has now. The most influential part of French society aired its views by word of mouth in the drawing-rooms of gifted or ambitious ladies. People like Mme. du Deffand or Mme. d'Épinay set aside one or two evenings every week for large parties at which the two most usual forms of entertainment were good food and brilliant talk. Sometimes there would be one evening for artists and one for *gens de lettres*. The *Philosophe* would attend one or more of these salons with more or less regularity: d'Holbach, the "personal enemy of God," was very rich and held his own. He entertained on Sundays and Thursdays and said things "à faire tomber le tonnerre sur sa maison." Montesquieu and Diderot, who talked even more brilliantly than they wrote, were able to make the most of the great opportunities offered them in the salons. There they often met Englishmen such as Horace Walpole, Hume or Gibbon, so that they not only spread their views among the upper classes in France, but were known in England too. Mme. Geoffrin, an exact contemporary of Voltaire's, entertained Stanislaus Augustus, the future King of Poland. Catharine II of Russia made overtures to her; Maria Theresa and Joseph II gave her a reception in Vienna. Mme. La Popélinière, the wife of a rich financier, was not so aristocratic. Her house was called "La Ménagerie" because she invited both bad company and good. The most philosophic salon of all was that of Mlle. de l'Espinasse. She decorated it with busts of d'Alembert and Voltaire and made it the "laboratory of the *Encyclopædia*."

Though by forming a public opinion the salons to some extent filled the place of modern newspapers, their influence did not reach beyond a comparatively small though influential circle. But the *Encyclopædia* educated the middle classes of France. Nothing except the *Dictionnaire Philosophique* of Voltaire reflects the unphilosophic teaching of the *Philosophes* more clearly than the *Encyclopædia*. It was a propagandist dictionary—in other words a contradiction in terms. It was a compendium of useful information, a commentary on current abuses, a programme of reform and the statement of a new religion. Its creed could be summarized in two articles of faith: "I believe in man," and "I believe in human progress." "L'homme est le terme unique d'où il faut partir, & auquel il faut tout ramener," said Diderot. "Abstraction faite de mon existence & du bonheur de mes semblables, qu'importe le reste de la nature?"[1] "Posterity," he said, "is for the philosopher what the other world is for the devout," and it was the aim of the *Encyclopædia* to bring this message home to all. A sentence in the Prospectus is its real

[1] *Encyclopédie*, article "*Encyclopédie*" (Paris, 1754, Vol. V).

dedication—" À la postérité et à l'être qui ne meurt point."[1]

The Abbé de St. Pierre had thought the continued existence of poets and artists a proof that the earth was still cumbered with "fainéants," and the Encyclopædists did but echo his naïve utilitarianism when they neglected art, æsthetics and philosophy and devoted the bulk of their thirty-five volumes to explanations of the strictly useful arts and sciences and to discussions of economic problems. To increase the usefulness of their work a dozen volumes were filled with clear and accurate illustrations of the machinery and processes described in the text. The contributors represented all branches of knowledge and included some of the most famous men of the day. At their head was Diderot, the versatile and courageous editor. Voltaire popularized Newton, d'Alembert supplied the mathematics and theology and a famous article on Geneva as well as the long "Preliminary Discourse"; Quesnai who was Mme. de Pompadour's physician wrote on agriculture, Turgot on economics, Buffon on natural history and Rousseau on music. Lighter subjects such as dress were also included, while the vast number of unsolicited contributions on the most diverse topics, often written by people with more enthusiasm than knowledge, were a serious embarrassment to the editor. He himself took immense pains to produce useful and accurate work, visiting workshops and forges and looms to master all the details of their machinery before he set out to explain it.

The lesson that the *Philosophes* taught still stands out from the pages of those heavy volumes, now so seldom opened except by the curious passer-by who fingers dusty piles of enchantment and rubbish in the book-boxes ranged along the quays of the Seine. The *Philosophes* said that war and unequal conditions were the two worst evils of mankind, and that the two

[1] Morley, *Diderot*, Vol. I, p. 146.

all-powerful remedies were legislation and education. Legislation was to sweep away inequalities and to perfect material life: education was to wean people from their prejudiced attachment to the unreasonable laws and customs of the past. Among the particular evils which they condemned were the game laws, the slave trade and the colonial tyranny. If the governments were willing, all would go well, for men are only " des espèces de singes qu'on peut dresser à la raison comme à la folie."[1]

Simple as their lesson was, the Encyclopædists did not always express it plainly. As they wanted to be read they could not altogether flout the censors. Their method was therefore often subtle rather than direct. Just as Montesquieu had attacked the evils of French society by exposing them through the innocent mouth of a Persian, so the Encyclopædists attacked orthodoxy through imaginary " seekers after truth " in China or Japan; and as Montesquieu had criticized France under the name of Persia, so the Encyclopædists confounded orthodoxy under the pretence of attacking paganism or heresy. If the arguments were equally applicable to both it did not require much intelligence to substitute one name for another. And, tongue in cheek, they would solemnly ask the old type of scholastic question, such as " Adam, le premier de tous les hommes, a-t-il été philosophe ? "[2] Thus superficial conformity veiled the rebellion of their thought. But by a hint here, a sneer there, and by rousing so much interest in the achievements and problems of this world that their readers forgot to worry about their chances in the next, the Encyclopædists undermined the influence of the old faith, and threatened to wield to good purpose the chief weapon let fall by the crooked hands of the Church—the control of public opinion.

Each volume as it appeared roused more enthusiasm

[1] Voltaire.   [2] Morley, *Diderot*, Vol. I, p. 201.

than the last, until the whole of thinking France, from the aristocracy of court and salon at one end to the " petite bourgeoisie " of the provinces at the other, knew the *Encyclopædia* and what it stood for. The existence of an educated middle class in France when the Revolution came was thus largely due to the work of the *Philosophes*. The enmity of Church and State, now sulkily detached, now actively hostile, helped to increase the fame of the work though hindering its production. In 1751 and 1752 the Sorbonne, the Archbishop of Paris, the Parlement and the Conseil du Roi all took action in various ways against the Encyclopædists who had also to reckon with the enmity of Jesuits and Jansenists. The Conseil du Roi ordered the first two volumes to be destroyed. After a lull of five years during which the *Encyclopædia* continued to appear, the storm was raised again. A commission of lawyers and theologians examined the work and the Conseil suppressed it. But thanks to Mme. de Pompadour and to two of the king's ministers, it was eventually completed, and the government pretended not to know that part of this forbidden publication had been printed at Paris. Meanwhile, the authors had shared the vicissitudes of their work. Helvétius retracted the obnoxious views he expressed in *l'Esprit* and went to Germany. D'Alembert gave up his connection with the *Encyclopædia*, worn out by persecution. Diderot, who had already spent three years in prison in expiation of his opinions, fled for a time, though he returned to his post and completed his undertaking.

If Voltaire was the most brilliant, Diderot (1713-1784) was the broadest and the most profound of the *Philosophes*. He more, than all the rest, proves kinship with the many-sided leaders of the Renaissance, with the versatile Leonardo, with the gently sceptical and tolerant Montaigne, with Bacon the utilitarian scientist, and above all with boisterous laughter-loving

Rabelais, holding the glass to hypocrites and shams. Not as great a man as any of these, but the legitimate descendant of their age and a powerful influence in his own.

He was a troublesome husband, but a most lovable and generous friend. In a generation as famous for its personal quarrels as for anything else, he forgave d'Alembert for deserting him and tried to avoid a rupture with Rousseau who had a genius for quarrelling with everyone. Like Rousseau he went through a period of squalid adversity, and received a most inadequate salary for his work on the *Encyclopædia*, but he was always ready to give his services to those who sought his help, and seems to have written parts of several books which appeared under other names. He even helped a young scoundrel, intent on blackmail, to publish with profit a satire against himself. His poverty failed either to embitter his outlook or to attach him to the flesh-pots necessary to Voltaire, for once he insisted on leaving a too comfortable post, saying " what I want is not to live better but to avoid dying."[1] But there was one experience he could not endure, and that was teaching a dull pupil.

Unlike Voltaire and Rousseau he was no dilettante. He was deeply interested in machinery, in physics and philosophy and music, and was an authority on literature, painting and the drama. A brilliant writer, he was a still more brilliant talker. Intellectually an open-eyed and honest sceptic he was incapable of prostituting his reason to his humanity as Voltaire had done. Neither would he sacrifice it to his love of life. He saw clearly that his materialistic philosophy led to atheism on the one hand; to a denial of immortality on the other. "Pourrir sous du marbre ou pourrir sous la terre c'est toujours pourrir." The world then was foolishness? Yes: " le monde est une sottise. Ah! la belle sottise pourtant." But with all his variety of occupa-

[1] Morley, op. cit., Vol. I, p. 20.

tion, his keen joy in experience, he was not deliberately seeking to circumvent the shortness of life, for with the unhurried dignity of the few who live up to a belief in eternity, he devoted twenty years of unsparing toil to the *Encyclopædia* which carried his influence into thousands of homes.

To-day we know him better by two short posthumous works, *La Religieuse* and *Le Neveu de Rameau*. *La Religieuse* is in many ways exactly the kind of book we should expect from the Voltairean *Philosophes*. The heroine, Sœur Sainte-Suzanne, is the embodiment of the ideal reason animating their ideally natural human being. Like Voltaire's characters in *Candide* she is only an automaton, fashioned not for life of her own but as a useful vehicle for the thoughts of her creator. She is innocent in word and deed, unselfish, forgiving and thinking no evil, kind to others, honest with herself. Above all she is the victim of environment. First her parents, then her confessor, then one convent after another force her to live a life for which she feels unfitted. Even the law is against her. When, after fruitless attempts, she at last escapes, it is only to be tormented by the fear of recapture, and we leave her exclaiming in defiant despair "il y a des puits partout." Throughout she is the helpless prisoner of circumstance, cajoled, terrorized, maltreated and shamefully used but never to be moved from her hopeless resolve to live her own life as reason and nature meant it to be. On the other hand Diderot shows with deeper psychological insight, though with more exaggeration, than the other *Philosophes* the evil of asceticism. In one convent the result of self-inflicted cruelty is a passion for cruelty towards others; in another the complete demoralization of the abbess and her nuns is the ultimate penalty of self-indulgence in a life where nature is denied. Asceticism is thus both foolish and wicked; foolish because it defeats its own ends, wicked because it hurts other people. "Why," he makes Rameau ask in *Le Neveu de Rameau*, do we so often see " les dévots si durs, si fâcheux, si insociables ? C'est qu'ils se sont imposé une tâche qui ne leur est pas naturelle." In a few lines he sketches unforgettably the daily life of an ascetic whose night is broken by outraged nature seeking to cast aside in dreams the burden imposed by the unnatural day. Elsewhere in the same book he condemns all suffering, whether self-inflicted or not, because it makes other people unhappy.

Diderot had plenty of accusations of the old kind to bring against the convents and the whole ecclesiastical hierarchy, complaints of their greed, their complaisance, their hypocrisy, their deliberate attempt to darken understanding. In *Le Neveu* he no longer attacks one part of the Church with the concentrated force of *La Religieuse*, but plays almost incidentally upon one scene after another of ecclesiastical life with the searchlight of his restless and vivid prose, here an instant, gone the next, but always flashing a clear-cut image into the mind's eye. Without once referring directly to the Jesuits he parodies their casuistry by letting Rameau prove that the proper use of good literature is to learn from it how to be a knave without talking like one; that as in every language there are exceptions to general rules of grammar, so in every trade there are exceptions (*idiotismes*) to the general rules of morality. One is equally entitled to use *idiotismes* of either sort : at all events one is merely doing what everyone else does, and why claim to be better than one's fellows ?

In *Le Neveu de Rameau* society is to Diderot what the Church was to Voltaire. Society is nothing but a vast sham, a counterfeit temple raised to a counterfeit god. It is built on the false foundation of inequality, this man surfeiting on the starvation of his neighbour. It has no intellectual interest beyond vulgar and malicious gossip, no aim but to get rich and to buy gross material pleasures. It knows no honour but wealth, "la ceinture dorée," and no sin but poverty. "Quoi qu'on fasse on ne peut se déshonorer quand on est riche."

Like the other *Philosophes* Diderot knew how to make people see an institution as it was, not as it appeared to be. But his condemnation of society went deeper than theirs. Like them he attacked specific abuses directly, from outside as it were. But at the same time he made a far more deadly indirect attack; for, working outwards from within, he left society to damn itself through the mouth of Rameau, the man it had defaced.

Rameau is the centre of the book. He is a living creature of flesh and blood, not an empty vessel for his author's wit, but a real man borrowed from life, and born again of Diderot's imagination and sympathy, and above all of his experience. Rameau is a villain with a good prospect of the gallows, but without being told so directly we are made to feel that here is a man, full of promise as nature made him, transformed into a criminal by the baseness of society, its low ideals, its unjust institutions. Rameau has genius, but society having no use for it, he is forced to pervert it to suit society in order to live. He justifies his parasitical existence, praises the lowest means of making money, confesses that he would behave like the rich if he could. Yet with it all he never quite loses our sympathy, not only because his light-hearted cynicism is vastly entertaining, but because he is the victim of circumstance and we find ourselves wondering if in his place we should not be the same. We may wonder, too, if we should still possess the intellectual honesty that Rameau never loses: he may deceive others, but he never stoops to deceive himself.

In breadth as in depth Diderot surpassed his fellows. If we can take *Le Neveu* as the final expression of his outlook on life we may doubt whether he ever attained a consistent philosophy, but we do see that he was ill-content with the superficial and narrow reasoning of the other *Philosophes*. Though none could have worked harder for the "philosophic" cause than himself, he could see its limitations. Between his hints of generous appreciation he pokes kindly fun through Rameau's mouth at all the *Philosophes* in turn, and at the movement they represent: "imaginez l'univers sage et philosophe; convenez qu'il serait diablement triste." In a book not intended for publication there would be no point in saying such things for the censor's benefit. In the same way, though passionately convinced of the goodness of nature, he sees the other side—that without education the natural baby would grow up into a repulsive man, that it is difficult to deny the truth of Rameau's picture of nature in which one species lives at the expense of another. Again, granted the usefulness of education, is it a panacea? Both Rameau and his philosopher friend are agreed that if a man is to know any one subject properly he must devote his whole life to it with no chance of ever having the time to teach it. Then is the evil plight of man within the power of human will to mend or end? Is not man, after all, in the grip of forces that cannot be conquered by legislation or by education? The question is not definitely put, but it is implied. And by this implication Diderot shows that the Renaissance faith in the will of man was ready for decay when the height of its flowering seemed at hand. Once admit the impotence of man and the way is left open for the superhuman; for the natural and supernatural forces of the Romanticists, the God of Rousseau and of Chateaubriand, the ghosts of Goethe and Sir Walter Scott, and the titanic storms of Victor Hugo.

It is clear, however, that Diderot had no suspicion that he might be shaking hands with Rousseau above the diminished head of human reason; the whole of his life, and indeed the general tenor of *Le Neveu* itself, contradicts such a suggestion. Hedged about by his unsolved questions Diderot stands with feet planted on the rock: "le point important est que vous et moi nous soyons, et que nous soyons vous et moi, que tout aille d'ailleurs comme il pourra." Even if we cannot alter the world we cannot condemn it entirely, because it produced us. Here at all events is solid fact, the last resort of the "philosophic" teaching, for it is only another way of saying "il faut cultiver notre jardin." And as we shut the book with the echo of Rameau's mocking laughter in our ears, two thoughts, sprung from this concentration of interest in mankind, gradually dominate the myriad ideas that the dialogue has raised—the first that hypocrisy is the only vice that utterly defaces a man, the second that large-hearted tolerance and practical kindness are the only indispensable virtues. Charity is better than genuis. "C'est un sublime ouvrage que Mahomet;[1] j'aimerais mieux rehabilité le mémoire des Calas."[2]

Closely connected with the loosely banded Encyclopædists was a more compact school of economic thinkers whose leader Quesnai had written the articles on agriculture in the *Encyclopædia*. They were known at first as the "Économistes," and later on as "Physiocrats." They were narrower and more conservative in their outlook than the Encyclopædists. Though they agreed with the Encyclopædists in demanding universal and compulsory education, they did not believe in the human origin of society, nor that complete equality of conditions was possible. They did not even object to the censors except when their own works were condemned. Their real interest was confined to economic problems and they only troubled their heads about government because they saw that the economic and political spheres of life could not be separated. Like the English Whigs, they thought

---

[1] One of Voltaire's plays.
[2] *See* below, p. 151.

that the one essential function of government was to protect property, but the liberty of which they dreamed was economic, not political. They believed that the world's happiness and the wealth of nations would be best attained by allowing nature to have its way unhindered in industry and commerce. They built up their economic theory on the half-truth that the land and those who develop and till it are the sole sources of wealth. This did not prevent much of their teaching from being of value. They did not affirm that manufacturing classes or mercantile states were wholly useless, and from this concession they finally concluded that agriculture and industry on one hand, agricultural and mercantile countries on the other, are interested each in the other's welfare. This belief reinforced their fundamental idea that nature, like any other machine, must be allowed to work, and led them to demand that trade should be freed from restrictions within each state, and that tariffs should be lowered or removed between different states. Here they flung down the gauntlet to the mercantilists, who wished by a multiplicity of regulations and tariffs to protect one industry from another, and to make each state completely self-sufficing and able to compete with other states in every field of manufacture.

Besides writing and talking, the *Philosophes* acted. And though with most of them deeds fell short of words, Voltaire freely spent his energy and fortune in running to earth specific abuses. His most famous deed of humanity was to restore honour to the name of Calas.

Calas was an old merchant who lived at Toulouse. He was a Protestant, but his youngest son was a Catholic. One day his elder son committed suicide. He was a wild and dissipated youth, but the Catholic clergy spread a rumour that he had been about to embrace the Catholic faith and that his father had strangled him on that account. So the suicide's corpse lay in state and performed miracles while the rest of the family were in prison. Then the old father was broken on the wheel, condemned to death without a shadow of evidence against him. His children were shut up in a monastery and forced to become Catholics.

Stung to the quick by this irrational cruelty, Voltaire moved heaven and earth to get the sentence reversed. He wrote his famous *Treatise on Tolerance*. He compelled the Council of State to demand the minutes of the trial from the Parlement of Toulouse. He was met with refusals and delays, but after three years' fighting he gained his point. The Toulouse sentence was pronounced unjust, the dead man's honour was restored, and damages were paid to his family.

This was only one of several cases of gross injustice which Voltaire investigated and remedied as far as he could, restoring their fair name to some and saving the lives of others. Sirven and young Étalonde, two innocent victims of religious intolerance, fled to him at Ferney where no one dared to molest them. One of his last deeds of humanity was to appeal against the unjust sentence that had condemned General Lally to death. And as he lay dying in the early summer of 1778 the news came that he had succeeded. He at once wrote to rejoice with the dead man's son. He may have been vain as a peacock, mean as a miser, snobbish as a flunkey, but here is a last effort of his pen.

> " Le mourant ressuscite en apprenant cette grande nouvelle; il embrasse bien tendrement M. de Lally; il voit que le roi est le défenseur de la justice; il mourra content."

Not the epitaph he would have chosen for himself; but had it adorned his tomb none could have failed to envy it or admit its truth.

The *Philosophes* also put their ideas into practice by visiting different courts and putting personal pressure on the rulers of Europe to make enlightened laws. Owing to the popularization of science and philosophy, eighteenth century sovereigns were easily accessible to thinkers. Some kings were genuinely interested, others counted on adding lustre to their crowns by appearing to be so. This made the *Philosophes* hopeful of securing " a few wise reigns." That done, the millennium would follow. Voltaire was only one of the many French savants who enlivened the court of Frederick the Great with their discussions and quarrels; Diderot visited Catharine II of Russia, who was also advised by the Économiste Mercier de la Rivière.

Faith in reason and the bright destiny of man partly accounted for this childlike confidence in laws and princes. Reason would dictate laws to sweep away the ancient institutions and traditions that alone hindered nature from flowering into a golden age. There was no necessity to invent the laws which would achieve this consummation; they were inherent and discoverable in nature, but they must be given fair play. " All human laws," said Burke, " are properly speaking only declarations. They may alter the mode and application, but have no power over the substance of original justice." The removal of old laws and other hindrances, however, could not be effected without the law-givers. And the law-givers of the age were for the most part autocratic monarchs. Moreover, in France the king was by tradition the defender of the people against the outworn institution of feudalism: he was the enemy of local tyranny and civil war. So it was but natural that the *Philosophes* should be true to the Renaissance faith in monarchy, in spite of their theoretical admiration of republics. Voltaire, much as he admired England, failed to appreciate the political liberty he found there. Condorcet, last and most extreme representative of the Encyclopædists, said in the year of revolution that "society is . . . exclusively itself the governing power. . . . In France . . . this power has been placed in the hands of the Prince. His person is sacred, because his authority is legitimate, and because he is the holder of the power of all the citizens, that he may execute the laws."

But if kings must be powerful to serve this great cause of liberating reason and making it law, they must remember that they are but instruments. They are not the masters, but the servants of their subjects whom they must enlighten by providing free education, by allowing freedom of speech, of writing and of conscience, and by administering reasonable punishment to those who act against the common good. In short, kings are to cultivate the reason of their people, to give it free scope, and to discourage those who disobey its sovereign voice. And to fulfil these functions, they must be wise, benevolent and supreme. Neither Physiocrat nor *Philosophe* could see any but a royal road to happiness, and though ultimately the French people thought they saw a shorter cut, the *Philosophes* first had their way, and Europe tried to reach the golden age by the regeneration of her kings.

CHAPTER VII

REGENERATE MONARCHY

"... je n'ai jamais bien compris les subtiles distinctions, sans cesse répétéés, sur les différentes formes de gouvernement. Je n'en connais que de deux espèces ; les bons et les mauvais : les bons, qui sont encore à faire ; les mauvais, dont tout l'art est, par différens moyens, de faire passer l'argent de la partie gouvernée dans la bourse de la partie gouvernante." Helvétius to Montesquieu.
(*Œuvres*, Paris, 1818, Vol. III, 263–264.)

"Pour être homme d'État, on ne doit pas cesser d'être homme."
D'Alembert, *Œuvres*, Vol. I, p. 37 (Paris, 1821).

"He that will erect a commonwealth against the judgment of Machiavel is obliged to give such reasons for his enterprise as must not go a-begging." Harrington.

"Joseph II dotted the i's of Luther's handwriting."
Figgis, *From Gerson to Grotius*, p. 15.

THE Age of Reason, then, dawned long before men raised an altar to her in the cathedral of revolutionary Paris. Hailed by thinkers in the seventeenth century, she became in the eighteenth the guide and handmaid of kings and ministers. At last enlightenment visited those who had not only the will but the power to apply wisdom to the government of states. Frederick the Great in Prussia, Joseph II in Austria, Catharine II in Russia, Leopold of Tuscany and Charles III of Naples in Italy, Turgot in France, Pombal in Portugal, Struensee in Denmark —all the great rulers and ministers of the age— flocked to the altar of the new deity. In the eighteenth century Plato need not have looked in vain for a philosopher king.

During this era, there was scarcely a king who would refuse to admit that it was his first duty to promote the welfare of his subjects. This new enthusiasm of crowned heads for rationalism and humanitarianism fitted the Renaissance conception of the state as a vast machine driven by the hand of its ruler. Humanitarianism dictated care for the ruled, but so does reason dictate care for the parts of a machine. Aggrandizement of the state is more possible where the people are contented, as a machine runs more smoothly when oiled. But as the parts of a machine cannot lubricate themselves and cannot choose their own functions, so the people ruled by a philosophic despot were held by him to be incapable of choosing the things that were for their good, or of defining their rights and duties. Everything must be done for them by the government; they must owe nothing to their own initiative. They might have equality but not liberty; they might have toleration but no racial or religious prejudices. This total neglect of the personal element was in the long run fatal to a régime designed to ensure the welfare and good behaviour of human beings and not of cog-wheels, but though the régime itself passed, it left behind it some permanent memorials of its good intentions.

In spite of essential differences between their tasks, their personalities and their achievements, the rulers of the eighteenth century pursued in the main the same ends and used the same means. At heart they were all trying to secure a strong centralized despotism; and though sincerely anxious to govern for the good of their people, they were, in general, guilty of assuming without proof that despotism was for the good of the people. To the kings despotism was an end; to the philosophers it was a means: to the kings the good of the people was a secondary consideration; to the philosophers it was a religion.

Some kings had more to do than others in order to

REGENERATE MONARCHY

secure the strong state they wanted, but every one of them except the king of France had to reform his government, that is the central executive. Wherever the old tradition of government by the advice of the nobility survived, it was abandoned for government by paid officials of the crown. Aristocracy was replaced by bureaucracy. Catharine of Russia, for example, continued and completed the policy begun by Peter the Great of relying for all governmental purposes on the services of a bureaucracy. All civil and military affairs of importance were concentrated in the hands of the Tsarina and her officials. Catharine kept the controlling voice in all such matters. In Prussia the same work of centralization was carried out by Frederick William I and completed by his son Frederick the Great. A General Directory composed of paid officials of the crown sat at Berlin and supervised the administration.

But it was useless merely to secure centralization at the seat of government. Local government, all over Europe in a state of extreme chaos, must be simplified and put under the control of the central bureaucracy. What the enlightened despots tried to create was a unified system of administration allowing much division of labour, but no local initiative. They would have admired the local government of modern France. They mapped out their countries into large districts, divided these into smaller districts which were generally sub-divided into still smaller units. These administrative areas were usually artificial and were intended to destroy local feeling and the ancient privileges of the towns. Each district was given its own governmental machinery, but no power to do anything of importance, such as the raising and spending of large sums of money, without the permission of the official in charge of the superior district. He in turn would be dependent on some higher official who would be subordinate to the central executive. This last could generally take no independent action without the sovereign's leave. Thus the smallest unit of local government had virtually no independent existence apart from the central government.

This unification of administrative systems was paralleled by the attempt to reform judicial systems on similar lines. In most countries there was not yet a single hierarchy of courts for the whole land, but a confused medley of jurisdictions arising from the sæcular struggle between aristocracy and Church and crown. It was the aim of the enlightened despots to substitute order for this chaos. In Austria, for instance, courts of three grades were instituted—courts of first instance, appeal and final revision. Feudal justice, where not extinguished, became a survival instead of a function.

This highly centralized governmental system, worked throughout by officials dependent on the crown, helped to eliminate the old forces of aristocracy. In Russia and Austria, it is true, the nobility were still powerful, but in Prussia they lost all political power.

There still remained the Church, that other age-long foe of secular despotism. All the enlightened despots aimed at making the Church merely a department of state. Catharine, following (for once) her husband's policy, continued to secularize Church lands, and in spite of dangerous opposition she made the orthodox Church dependent on the state, all the clergy becoming paid servants of the government. Frederick and his father succeeded equally well and with less difficulty, though when the latter interfered with ritual he met with opposition. Otherwise the Prussian clergy were submissive.

In the Austrian Empire, Joseph II tried to apply a similar policy. In his own words he "desired the bishops to become the recipients of wages, so that the Church might be in fact only one of the numerous departments of the state."[1] In 1783 he instituted

[1] Bright, *Joseph II*, p. 137.

civil marriage and divorce; and to sever the Church from all ties except that of the state he risked a separation with Rome, being "rather surprised and hurt by the extreme enthusiasm"[1] with which his subjects greeted Pius VI when he visited Vienna to protest against Joseph's Patent of Tolerance. He would not allow such of the monasteries as he did not suppress to continue their connection with foreign members of their Orders, and before his mother's death, he persuaded her to agree to the suppression of the Jesuits. Freedom of conscience was part of his centralizing policy. " Once grant freedom of belief," he said to his mother, " and there will be but one religion, that of directing all the citizens equally towards the good of the state . . . if only the State be duly served, if the laws of nature and society meet with reverence and the Supreme Being fail not of honour—why should you seek a wider sphere of influence?"[2] In 1781 he issued a Patent of Tolerance which gave citizenship and freedom of worship to Christian dissenters.

Even where such internal policies were successful, rulers felt the need of stabilizing despotism by external aggression. And a policy of external aggression involves the formation and upkeep of large and efficient armies. Thus all the enlightened despots, especially those who like Frederick and Joseph had extensive frontiers to defend, were keenly interested in army reform. To Frederick the Great and his father, the army was the core of policy. Prussian soldiers were poorly paid and cruelly disciplined, but their comfort was considered; all the nobles were forced to spend their best years in army service, but military rank conferred a prestige given by no other occupation, so that if the aristocracy lost their political power they retained their social prestige. In Russia, Catharine relied on her officers in all those matters where the civil bureaucracy could not serve her. In Austria, Maria Theresa reorganized

[1] *Ib.*, 139.   [2] *Camb. Mod. Hist.*, Vol. VI, p. 628.

her army, which had not been improved between the close of the Thirty Years War and Frederick's conquest of Silesia. Before her death she gave supreme command of the army to her son Joseph, and for the rest of his life its improvement was his chief hobby.[1]

But an army is an expensive luxury and raises the problem of finance. Catharine completely failed to cope with the financial difficulties of Russia—her army was large, her wars frequent, her extravagance phenomenal, and she left Russian finances in an even worse state than that in which she had found them. Joseph, on the other hand, improved the financial position of Austria, and saved the state from the bankruptcy which had threatened it on his accession. Frederick William and Frederick the Great were still more successful. Partly owing to the success of their centralized system of government, which depended upon the Councillors of Taxes, and partly owing to their strict economy they amassed a treasure of enormous size in proportion to the wealth of the country. The Prussian court was as economical as Catharine's was extravagant, and thrift was carried almost to excess by Frederick and his father. Frederick William was accustomed to thrust his arms into oversleeves to save the expensive cloth of his uniform when he was writing, and when Frederick the Great once received half a dozen pairs of wrist-ruffles, he slit them horizontally, thus making a dozen pairs. "See," he exclaimed, " how I make something out of nothing." That was his aim all through his life—to make something out of nothing, and he sometimes pursued it ungenerously, as when he allotted the worst land to the foreign immigrants whom he had attracted to Prussia by specious promises.

It was natural that in striving to direct the political life of their states, the enlightened despots should wish to control their economic life as well. Here on the

[1] Bright, *Joseph II*, p. 177.

whole they parted company with the Physiocrats, who were urging that the laws of nature should be allowed free play in the economic sphere no less than in jurisprudence. In France and England, the Physiocrats did have appreciable influence. Turgot, who said he was neither an Encyclopædist nor an Économiste, had much sympathy with their teaching, and when he became Louis XVI's minister he put into effect as many of their ideas as his short tenure of office allowed. He freed both the corn trade and the wine trade from restrictions and deprived the gilds of their industrial monopoly. In England there was less need of internal reform, and even in commercial policy there had been a free trade element since the beginning of the eighteenth century.[1] Chatham was the last of the great mercantilist statesmen. His son, influenced by the writings of Adam Smith, who while pointing out the fallacies of the Physiocrats, was in close touch with their leaders, came forward as the champion of the new liberal ideas. The upshot was that France and England met as Physiocrats to sign the commercial treaty of 1786. This treaty, doomed to failure by the outbreak of the Revolution, was nevertheless one of Pitt's greatest achievements. It is interesting, too, as a practical outcome of the intellectual alliance between France and England which survived unimpaired through all the wars and rivalries that fill the political annals of the two nations during the greater part of the eighteenth century. In Russia, Catharine was prevailed upon to free industry and trade from certain restrictions, and to allow the export of bullion.

But this was all. Catharine reverted to the mercantilist policy which most of the kings never forsook. Over by far the greater part of pre-revolutionary Europe strict governmental control of trade and industry was maintained.

To encourage industry at home, mercantilist policy

[1] Hewins, *English Trade and Finance*, p. 129 ff.

162 FROM RENAISSANCE TO REVOLUTION

moved in two apparently opposite directions—one of which the Physiocrats would have approved. On the one hand, for example, rulers aimed at removing the hindrances to industrial development implied in the now perverted gild system; on the other, they imposed strict governmental supervision and interference. The gilds did not disappear for many years: they survived for instance in many parts of nineteenth century Germany, but they became quasi-governmental institutions in the more centralized states. In a word, sectional restriction was reduced, but only to be replaced by state regulation.

This was the case to a greater or less extent in all the countries ruled by the philosopher kings, but nowhere was the system so complete as in the Prussia of Frederick William I and of Frederick the Great. The Prussian Councillors of Taxes, who were the chief agents of local administration, supervised every department of local life. They had to fix weights and measures, to examine the quality of beer, to attract capital to the towns, to supervise and encourage every advance of industry and commerce and even to discourage immorality and idleness. They were not unlike the chief functionaries of the mediæval gilds, except that they were crown officials. It was on their recommendation that state subsidies would be granted to this or that infant industry—and in Prussia, considering the poverty of the country, subsidies were granted with a lavish hand. Frederick built factories in Berlin and handed them over to manufacturers, and to encourage the Silesian linen industry a loom was given free to every immigrant weaver. Under his rule every trade had to submit to the most minute regulations. He was not above issuing an order to discourage maidservants from lighting their fires with rags which were needed for the paper industry.[1]

[1] The rags were burned for tinder. Frederick said that the ragmen were to give touchwood to the maids in exchange for rags. *Camb. Mod. Hist.*, Vol. VI, p. 719.

It was useless, however, for governments to try to promote manufacture and industry if there were not sufficient people to do the work. The encouragement of immigration had been part of the policy of Prussian rulers from the seventeenth century onwards, and in the eighteenth century both Catharine and Frederick held out every inducement to foreigners to settle on their sparsely peopled territory.

Another vital necessity for the growth of trade and industry and also for the rapid movement of troops was the improvement of communications. Perhaps France and England, the Low Countries and Northern Italy were the only countries in Europe where road-building had made any progress since the fall of the Roman Empire, and Arthur Young's execrations show that even in England the art left much to be desired. In France, though the main roads were good, the cross-roads were bad. In Russia the problem was almost hopeless, but Catharine did what she could to facilitate intercourse by making canals. Frederick and Joseph built roads as well as canals, and Frederick sank much wealth in draining marshes and clearing forests. For the improvement of foreign trade, enlightened despots made great efforts to develop merchant shipping and to obtain good roadsteads.

Thus all over continental Europe rulers were interesting themselves to some purpose in matters small and great in order to further the material prosperity of their countries. And though they reckoned wealth rather in terms of bullion, armies and territory than in terms of human well-being and happiness, they did honestly care for what they considered to be the interests of their subjects. Frederick the Great called himself a republican and the " King of Beggars," and was probably sincere in considering himself the first servant of the state. An inhuman rationalism did not prevent Joseph II from having a warm love for the poor and weak, from being deeply distressed by the havoc wrought among his peasants by armies and from wishing to be known as "The Lover of Mankind" (Der Schätzer der Menschen) rather than as "Holy Roman Emperor." Catharine, too, though of harder composition than Joseph, shared in common with all the enlightened despots a wish to make life easier for the poor, and the punishment of criminals less barbarous. Joseph abolished serfdom, and Catharine appears to have wished to do the same in Russia, but the interests of the nobles were too strong for her. Frederick abolished slavery in West Prussia, his first instalment of Polish territory. Throughout the greater part of Europe the use of torture was forbidden during this age, prison conditions were improved, and penal codes made more merciful. All the enlightened rulers wanted equal justice for rich and for poor and most of them tried to codify the laws of their dominions in order to simplify them and to bring them into accord with the ideas of the time. The fame of the Napoleonic Code has made people forget that the Allgemeine Landrecht of Frederick the Great came first, and that it was the greatest achievement of its kind since the days of Justinian. In Russia, Catharine attempted the colossal work of codifying and modernizing Russian laws. But after some years she abandoned a task undertaken too lightheartedly, with little or no previous preparation, and entrusted to men of insufficient ability.

The general belief of the enlightened despots that it was their duty to further the welfare of their subjects led to educational reforms. Frederick founded academies and freed the press in a country where his father had issued an edict introducing compulsory education. Joseph II tried to emancipate education from its ecclesiastical trammels: "The State is no cloister," he said, "and we have, in good truth, no monks for our neighbours."[1] He founded for the clergy schools

[1] *Camb. Mod. Hist.*, Vol. VI, p. 628.

which he placed under the authority of the state. In 1781 he abolished the censorship. Catharine delivered herself of the opinion that " education is at the root of all good and evil," and though her hope that each province should have its national school and that new universities should be founded remained a pious wish, she did found schools both for boys and for girls.

Closely connected with this desire to hold in their hands not only the strings of government and commerce but also the threads of thought, was the interest taken in the development of the arts and sciences by the philosopher kings.

The trouble was that they could only receive censored journals from France, the home of culture. The *Philosophes* helped them over this difficulty by writing private journals of their own. The most famous of these was the *Correspondance Littéraire* edited by Grimm and Diderot. The *Correspondance* was a secret periodical written in manuscript and issued twice a month, and its subscription list included the names of Frederick the Great, Catharine II, the Queen of Sweden and the Grand Duke of Tuscany.[1] It contained candid and impartial criticism of the literature, art, drama and music of France and England, explanations of all the latest scientific discoveries such as inoculation, and a liberal spice of piquant anecdotes and scandal about all the notable people of the age. Politics were theoretically taboo, but discussions of toleration, education and finance were included. Its religious tone was agnostic but not militant; and as might be expected, it opened a subscription list for the Calas family.

The *Correspondance Littéraire* did for the courts of Europe what the *Encyclopædia* did for the middle classes of France, and it certainly did not leave the

[1] For this and the rest of the paragraph see S. G. Tallentyre, *The Friends of Voltaire*.

enlightened despots contented with a merely academic interest in culture. Frederick founded an opera-house in Berlin, and did his best to write poetry; Catharine allowed herself to be inoculated; Joseph offered the Chair of Medicine at Padua to Tissot, the famous physician of Lausanne, who denounced the overfeeding of invalids and who once danced a minuet with Gibbon. Invitations were showered by Frederick and Catharine on men of science and letters. Catharine made Diderot a colonel, much to Frederick's amusement, and also a councillor of state; and when he was at his wits' end for money, she bought his library and made him librarian, giving him fifty years' salary in advance. She never stood on ceremony with him, and when he was in Paris one of his duties was to buy the imperial rouge and sweets.

This attempt to make their courts the centre of culture had its counterpart in the energy with which the monarchs of this age travelled about their dominions. Catharine and Frederick were untiring in their zeal to collect first-hand information on all subjects connected with their work of ruling, and Joseph loved to pass in and out among his people dressed as one of themselves.

Directly or indirectly, this striving to make the court the centre of national life, this minute regulation of trade and industry, this artificial stimulation of commerce and manufacture, this improvement of social conditions, this zeal for education and enlightenment, this hostility to sectional interests, this reorganization of administrative and judicial systems, all served one purpose, namely the concentration of all the threads of government in the hands of the ruler.

In Prussia this task was comparatively easy, since by Frederick's time the country was fairly compact and the racial differences were not highly developed. Moreover, Prussia had been created by the government, so that neither the Church nor the aristocracy had a strong or decentralizing influence. Even Frederick's employment of French bureaucrats, though disliked, was tolerated. In Austria, however, Joseph's task was difficult. The central government was weak, race prejudice was violent, the power of the Church was strong. All the races of which the Empire was composed,—Germans, Czechs, Slavs and Magyars,—were jealous of each other and especially of Austria. Joseph's grandfather, Charles VI, had appeased the racial feeling of the Magyars by giving to Hungary certain rights and privileges which were the foundation of the modern Dual System that lasted till 1918. When Joseph tried to introduce some sort of order and simplicity into the chaotic and cumbrous machine of imperial government and to subordinate provincial interests to the interests of the whole state, his people became suspicious that he was using the imperial position to further Austria's aims. Joseph's failure was no marvel. No one ever solved the racial problem of the Austro-Hungarian Empire. And Joseph took the best means to fail. Dominated by the voice of reason, he saw no sense in racial prejudice. Therefore he ignored it, and treated the various nationalities as he would treat the various regiments of his army. Consequently the Hungarians hated him and withstood him successfully when he tried to supersede their Diet and their national distinctions of race, language and religion ; and his far-away Belgian subjects revolted against him under similar provocation and in the same conservative spirit. In the same way and for the same reasons he failed in his ecclesiastical policy. That Joseph failed to eradicate their unreasonable religious prejudices from his people's minds was perhaps fortunate for him. He did not realize that if he succeeded in destroying the strength of the Church he would be postponing still further the realization of a unified empire, for religion was one of the few ties that held his conglomerate inheritance together.

In spite of the vastness of her dominions Catharine had apparently an easier task than Joseph. The central government had already been brought under despotic control by Peter the Great, and, on the other hand, the non-Russian provinces lacked that tradition of national self-government which spurred the Magyars to resist Joseph's centralizing policy.

It was not only, however, differences in the nature of their tasks that determined the success or failure of the philosopher kings. Differences in character had a share in determining the results of their reigns. Frederick and Catharine, seeing clearly and cynically the discrepancies between the humanitarian and selfish aims of despotism, were hard-headed enough to be advocates of reason and enlightenment only when it suited their interests. Catharine was a German Lutheran, but, once in Russia, she threw off traditions of race and religion as easily as she would slip out of a cloak that proved cumbersome. Again, both she and Frederick saw scant reason in the national feeling of the Poles when they wished to partition their land. But when it suited them to weaken Poland, they insisted that the unreasonable and traditional methods of Polish government should be maintained. Frederick the Great, in spite of his vaunted enthusiasm for equality, upheld firmly the old mediæval system of rigid class divisions because, however unreasonable such divisions were, upon them depended, in his view, the stability of the Prussian state. Consequently he did his best to save the lands of the peasant proprietors from being absorbed by the owners of large estates. This capacity to base one's reasoning on the unreason of human nature was foreign to Joseph's mind. Had he lived to-day he might have found a safe vocation in enthusiastic propaganda work for Esperanto: in his own day his policy of trying to force all his subjects to speak one language was more dangerous. Joseph made philosophy his sovereign while the others made her their handmaid, and she proved a better servant than mistress.

It is difficult to measure the success of the Enlightened Despots. Catharine's success was but superficial. She might and did secure the ascendancy of a bureaucratic and military caste dependent on the crown; she might and did in moments of aggression achieve the illusion that she was leading one single nation to conquest and glory. But between the governing class and the Russian peoples a great gulf still lay fixed, so that, except superficially, Russia made no approach to the ideal eighteenth century state in which all the people formed one commonwealth, where all particular interests were subordinated to the interest of the whole, and where the nature of those interests and the best means of pursuing them were decided by the king and by the king alone.

Indeed none of the eighteenth century states approximated, though Prussia and Tuscany made some approach, to this ideal. The aggressive policy, alone, of the enlightened rulers made the internal welfare of their states impossible. In the first place war can only benefit sections of a people. In the second place the conduct of wars, and in peace the upkeep of large armies require much money which might otherwise be devoted to purposes in which the whole nation is interested. Thus Catharine and Frederick might have the best will in the world on the matter of public education, but however good their intentions, however enlightened their schemes, little could be done in the way of providing and endowing schools and universities while the resources of their countries were being drained to finance wars and troops. Again, heavy taxation in Prussia, and complete financial chaos in Russia were the result of the aggressive policies of their rulers. Consequently, everywhere, though more especially in Russia, the advance in social enlightenment and in the general welfare of the people was to a large extent illusory.

The chasm between government and people, so apparent in Russia, existed to a greater or less degree in all countries, for the rulers made the mistake of confusing the government with the state, of thinking they could regenerate the latter by remodelling the former.

The truth is that though there is nothing inherently antagonistic between the ideals of despotism and humanitarianism, the two are not generally good bedfellows. Homage to reason, service to humanity were paid, but in general only when the claims of enlightenment and philanthropy did not clash with the other more selfish interests of despotism.

Monarchy was not the only exponent of enlightenment. The Aufklärung was a European movement, and only because despotism was the most usual form of government did the new state-activities seem to be a monoply of crowned heads. The only considerable governments of pre-revolutionary Europe which were not monarchies were Great Britain and Holland. In these countries, it is true, many of the reforms associated on the Continent with the names of the philosopher kings had been already carried out in the sixteenth and seventeenth centuries. We have already seen how seventeenth century Holland led the way in economic policy and achievement, and how England, by virtue of her comparative freedom from foreign wars, was in the best position to follow in the footsteps of the Dutch in agriculture, trade, industry and finance. In the treatment of poverty the Dutch were the pioneers, and the English followed. Under Charles I the administration of the Poor Law reached a higher level of efficiency and humanity than was attained on the Continent, where, except in Holland, the problems of poverty and unemployment received inadequate attention until long after the age of the philosopher kings. In England, too, the censorship of the press had been abolished in 1695. Reason and humanity had gained a footing in the English Church as well as in English law. Toleration, as far as it went, was probably more effective than in less civilized countries such as Prussia where it was ostensibly more complete. The English clergy sought comfort rather than truth, and were therefore not fanatical. If the Nonconformists, now freed from persecution, slackened their religious zeal, they were the more amenable to reason. There was thus no need for the drastic anticlericalism of Voltaire. The English Deists taught that the individual human reason was an infallible tribunal to which each man must appeal in deciding between right and wrong, they deprived God of omnipotence and reduced him to the position of their own constitutional monarchs who reigned but did not govern. But though this teaching might lead to the atheism of Hume, the majority of thinking Englishmen, whatever their private opinions might be, were members of the official Church.

There was still, however, even in England, a large field for philanthropy and enlightenment. Hogarth's pictures show that the fine achievement of Whig civilization was floating above a poisonous gin-swamp. In the big towns the housing and clothing of the poor were squalid and filthy: infant mortality was incredibly high. Prisons were revolting, and crime was the natural accompaniment of misdemeanour when capital punishment was prescribed for both. In London the police system was so bad that the public had virtually to come to terms with the criminal classes, and no one who has read Fielding's novels can preserve any illusions about the Justices of the Peace.

As compared with continental states England was in some respects backward and even retrograde. If in 1800 more than two hundred crimes were punishable by death, " two-thirds of these had been added in the eighteenth century."[1] The English system of local government was "a chaos of authorities, a chaos of jurisdictions . . . a chaos . . . of areas" until fifty years ago. Semi-barbaric Prussia could boast an edict prescribing compulsory education a full century before Forster's Education Act was passed, and "Hardwicke's Marriage Act" made no provision for civil marriage. The Playhouse Act of 1737 was opposed by Lord Chesterfield as a revival of the press censorship because it required the licence of the Lord Chamberlain for the production of plays.

Though reforms were made, the influence of the Aufklärung on English legislation was small. Reason and utility might be the private standards of the governing classes, but they did not translate them into law. Walpole's scepticism and tolerance hid behind formal orthodoxy and political opportunism. He refused to repeal the Test and Corporation Acts, though after 1727 dissenters could take shelter under the annual Act of Indemnity. Even if English governments had felt a passion for reform in the abstract they could not have enforced ideal legislation upon a backward people as the autocratic governments of the Continent could do. In the middle of the century, for instance, an act was passed allowing the naturalization of Jews. It was vigorously supported by the Bishops, but the popular outcry was so loud as to cause its repeal. On the other hand, when enlightened laws were made it was because public opinion had outstripped the law's conservatism. In 1736 the statutes against witchcraft were repealed, and in 1772 the use of judicial torture was abolished, but by the eighteenth century neither torture nor the persecution of witches was a practical evil. The most famous humanitarian work of the age was done in the last quarter of the century, that is after Wesley's religious revival had stimulated public opinion in a way that the

[1] C. Grant Robertson, *England under the Hanoverians*, p. 484, n.

Aufklärung had never done. John Howard was not a Deist but a Quaker. Robert Raikes, the educational pioneer, founded Sunday Schools. The abolition of the Slave Trade, achieved in 1807, but fought for in the previous century, was an Evangelical triumph. Again, it is probable that the more generous administration of the Poor Law that followed the Speenhamland decision of 1795 was due rather to economic pressure than to abstract principles of humanity. In the end, it is true, English law was forcibly apprenticed to reason and humanity by Jeremy Bentham. But Bentham was not born till 1748, he wrote nothing till nearly a generation later, and it was not until the nineteenth century that his influence had practical effect on legislation.

The English attitude towards letters and philosophy in the eighteenth century gives the key to the nature of the Aufklärung in England. Unlike France, Germany and Russia, England offered an asylum and not a gilded career to men of letters. Voltaire and Rousseau found in England a tolerance and safety that were more in accord with reason than the atmosphere of literary acrimony and personal spite that they had to breathe in the court society of Europe. Voltaire exclaimed that he could say aloud in London things that he dared not whisper in Paris. But neither he nor his friends were flattered by royal favours nor enticed to court. Under Anne and George I, it is true, men of literary fame had posts and sinecures showered upon them, but though Walpole's friend Queen Caroline delighted to surround herself with thinkers and scholars she died in 1737, and Walpole greatly diminished governmental patronage.

The point is that in England the court was not, as on the Continent, the centre of national life. The real rulers of England during the greater part of the century were the Whig aristocracy—" that most enviable of all the aristocracies of history, the men and women who look out from the canvases of Reynolds and Romney with a divine self-satisfaction bred of unchallenged possession of all that was really best in a great civilization."[1] These no less than the entirely different Diderot inherited the Renaissance faith in the power of the human will. They felt the charm of philosophy, learning and art. They made fine collections of famous pictures. Statesmen read Homer and Virgil, Livy and Tacitus, as a relaxation in their hours of leisure. Orators addressed a House of Commons that could appreciate the classical allusions and quotations which adorned their speeches—that would have shuddered with no simulated dismay at the sound of a false quantity.

The philosophic kings of England, then, were the Whigs. But though their culture came from the Renaissance, their politics did not. They would naturrally brook no bureaucracy such as those beloved of the enlightened despots abroad. They were not interested in the simplification of local government; they would have dismissed the notion of compulsory education as soon as entertained. Their governmental attitude was feudal and patriarchal rather than Renaissance and despotic; and their views seem to have permeated the minds of all those set in authority from the highest to the lowest. It is a duty imposed by God to be kind and generous to the poor, but the poor are to regard everything done for them by the rich as favours, not as rights. The daily prayer of the poor might be

> " God bless the Squire and his relations
> And keep us in our proper stations."

Hannah More explains this point of view to some villagers who had just been suffering from famine. After pointing out that they were better off than the inhabitants of many other villages because they had

[1] G. M. Trevelyan, *Lord Grey of the Reform Bill*, p. 16.

REGENERATE MONARCHY

" suffered no scarcity of religious instruction " she reminds them " that probably that very scarcity [1] has been permitted by an all-wise and gracious Providence to unite all ranks of people together, to show the poor how immediately they are dependent upon the rich. . . . It has also enabled you to . . . observe the benefits flowing from the distinction of rank and fortune, which has enabled the high so liberally to assist the low. . . . We trust the poor in general, especially those that are well instructed, have received what has been done for them as a matter of favour, not of right —if so, the same kindness will, I doubt not, always be extended to them, whenever it shall please God so to afflict the land."[2]

This refusal to admit that the poor had any capacity or any right to think or act for themselves, that whatever the rich gave them out of their superfluity was all that the Almighty intended them to have, brings us back to the root condemnation of eighteenth century government. What in England the rich tried to instil into the minds of the poor, the continental governments made the first maxim of state in dealing with all classes. The result was that the ideal of enlightened despotism failed even if and where it was realized. In Prussia, the scene of its greatest success, it concentrated the threads of government in the hands of one man to such an extent that chaos ensued at his death; it stultified the initiative of the Prussian people for several generations, it demoralized them by exaggerating their sense of dependence on the government. An English observer said that Prussia reminded him of a great prison with Frederick the Great as a gaoler amid his subjects as captives.[3]

---

[1] i.e. the material scarcity.
[2] *The Town Labourer*, 1760–1832, J. L. and B. Hammond, pp. 228–229.
[3] *See* H. W. V. Temperley, *Frederick the Great and Kaiser Joseph*, p. 21.

To us, the national democratic state, sovereign by virtue of anything rather than efficiency, common sense or humanity, seems the culmination of Renaissance monarchy. This is true, but it is only true because the political theory of the Renaissance never quite fitted the facts. If it had—if Louis XIV and Joseph II had really persuaded their people to want efficient government more than any other thing, and if they themselves had really been humanitarian—there is no reason to suppose that the national and democratic state system of the twentieth century need have followed.

The Voltairean conception of the state was a logical consequence of Renaissance theory. The *Philosophes* looked upon states as artificial administrative areas in which a certain number of human beings were grouped, not because of racial, religious, linguistic or historical bonds, but for the convenience of being governed. According to this idea, states are different in degree but not in kind from the modern French " arrondissement " or the English " union." People of one state are stupid to dislike being conquered by another, provided they are exchanging bad government for good. That is why the *Philosophes* applauded the spoliation of benighted Poland by the wise rulers of Prussia, Russia and Austria.

Moreover some thinkers, including the Abbé de St. Pierre, thought that people would only need a little education to see that a pan-European peace-league, led by France, was both natural and feasible. Administrative areas usually settle their differences without bloodshed, and no one could be so foolish as to resent the political chairmanship of France since Europe had already enrolled itself under her social and intellectual banner. Even Kant, who broke away from eighteenth century tradition, wanted Europe to become a federation. With the exception of the peace-league idea, this mechanical theory of the state was held rather as an assumption than as a definite doctrine, which shows more clearly than anything else how closely it seemed to fit the facts. And to some extent it did fit them. It fitted the cosmopolitan interests and habits of the upper classes; it fitted the European extent of French culture. It also fitted the energy with which the enlightened despots were hammering their dominions into the shape of administrative areas.

If this had been all, Europe might have developed as the *Philosophes* expected—into a continent divided into administrative areas ruled by autocratic monarchs, who might one day confer together under the presidency of the French king to guide humanity into the path of prosperity and peace. This would have been the natural result of fulfilling the promise of the Renaissance—of humanizing the state on principles of common sense.

But the Renaissance tradition decayed before this last fruition was achieved. Stronger than kings and upper classes and common sense were the " unreasonable " sentiments that Joseph and the *Philosophes* could not destroy—the religious and constitutional prejudices that never slept, the cultural traditions that slept but never died, and above all the fledgling pride of nationality which pre-revolutionary Europe did not recognize and could never have understood.

Perhaps the contrast between the superficial political system handed down from the Renaissance and the underlying causes of its destruction is most clearly illustrated by the effect of the American rebellion on Europe. Benjamin Franklin suggested to one of his correspondents that Europe might profit by the example of the United States to form a confederation of its own. If European civilization had really been what the *Philosophes* supposed, it is at least possible that the constructive achievement of the American rebels might have made a deep impression in Europe, especially as no one knew until long afterwards[1] of the storm and stress and compromise that lay behind the constitution. But in actual fact it was the destructive work of the Americans that most affected Europe—the overthrow of British dominion. It was this that fired the French revolutionaries with the ideal of triumphant liberty, that stimulated them to destroy and not to enlarge the Renaissance heritage which Voltaire had defended.

[1] A bare report of the proceedings was published in 1819, but the full story was not known till 1840 when Madison's notes were published by Congress.

CHAPTER VIII

CONCLUSION

" Il n'y a plus de patrie : je ne vois, d'un pôle à l'autre, que des tyrans et des esclaves."
Diderot, Neveu de Rameau, 87 (ed. Nilsson).

" Défiez vous de ces cosmopolites qui vont chercher au loin dans leurs livres des devoirs qu'ils dédaignent de remplir autour d'eux. Tel philosophe aime les Tartares, pour être dispensé d'aimer ses voisins." Rousseau, *Émile*, Bk. I (Paris, 1802, Vol. I, p. 23).

" Tout au contraire des théologiens, les médecins et les philosophes n'admettent pour vrai que ce qu'ils peuvent expliquer, et font de leur intelligence la mesure des possibles."
Rousseau, *Confessions*, Bk. VI (Berlin, 1921, Vol. II, p. 42).

IF Renaissance monarchy never became humane, neither did Renaissance culture. As in Elizabethan times the Renaissance had only enfranchised men of genius or wealth or good birth, so the eighteenth century culture descended from it was one of quality not quantity. The English aristocracy, the court society in Prussia and Russia, and even the salons of France with all their humanitarianism, their plea for freedom and equality of opportunity, were from this point of view only a stage more humane than Athenian culture had been with its foundation of slavery. The French Encyclopædists tried to make the Renaissance ideal of liberty the privilege of the many instead of the few ; unlike the English Whigs they aimed to bring the best in civilization to the average man of scanty leisure and shallow purse. In the *Encyclopædia* the article on " Journeyman " runs as follows :—" Journeyman—

a workman who labours with his hands and is paid day-wages. This description of men forms the great part of a nation ; it is their lot which good government ought to keep principally in sight. If the journeyman is miserable, the nation is miserable." But just as they failed on the whole to control the machinery of state in the interests of humanity, the *Philosophes* failed also to control more than a section of the public opinion of Europe. They disarmed the Church, but could not replace it, because they took a superficial estimate of the breadth and depth of human needs.

The hard-won belief of the Renaissance that man is sufficient unto himself, that the human will is omnipotent, was of untold value in restoring human self-respect after the close of the Middle Ages, and was justified by the scientific, philosophic and political achievements of the seventeenth century. But it was never more than a half-truth. And it was never credible to more than a select minority. Without material comfort or mental enlightenment, it was impossible for the most stoical English miner or Polish serf to rejoice in the achievements of a civilization which he did not share, or to believe in the power of his own will to remedy his state. The Church, at least to the devout, offered consolation for the present and substantial hopes for the future. But the religion of posterity preached by the Encyclopædists gives but cold comfort to most people, who are more interested in looking forward to a possible heaven that they hope to enter than to a certain posterity which they know they will never see.

It is often said that the Encyclopædists failed because they appealed to reason and neglected the emotions. This is not quite true. Voltaire thought the capacity for falling in love the only consolation for the miseries of life, and Diderot claimed that the passions are the best part of human nature because they are most creative. He not only fell in love with three women in succession, but gloried in his changeable nature. He was scarcely less barefaced than Rousseau in the enjoyment of his own sensation, whether sad or gay. But where Rousseau was content to enjoy, the Voltaireans must analyse cause and effect,—must explain everything scientifically if possible, but at any rate to satisfy common sense. What they neither understood nor allowed for was the spiritual and imaginative side of human nature—the passionate denial that the noblest longings and ideals have a purely material origin, the craving to know something more than common sense can tell, the faith that finds truth in paradox. The *Philosophes* could not understand the sublime poverty of St. Francis nor the "grand deaths" of those who perish for an idea. Neither did they feel the spiritual appeal of nature. Nature was not ignored by them. Voltaire often refers with pleasure to the lovely flowers in his Swiss garden, to his magnificent view of Lac Léman and the Alps, to the pleasant quietness of country life; and the Encyclopædists were as insistent as the Romanticists in appealing for a return to nature. But their conception of nature was different. Voltaire's vinegary allusions to the turmoil of Paris may have a tincture of the sour grape about them. His instinctive attitude towards the flowers in his garden and his view of the Alps was that of the eighteenth century proprietor. Mont Blanc could not awe him any more than his flowers could give him "thoughts that do often lie too deep for tears." Yet he wept almost as often as he fell ill. Frederick the Great was not far behind him. But how different were the simple tears of the "Aufklärung" from the transcendental dew of the Romanticists! When Maria Theresa accepted a share of Poland, Frederick said of her, "she wept and she took." Chateaubriand said of himself, "I wept and believed."

The eighteenth century view of history both in

France and England is a curious commentary on this failure to plumb the spiritual and imaginative depths of human life. The result of erecting a philosophy on common sense was a profound respect for facts. It seemed as if the fate of a doctrine or institution hung upon the truth or falsity of its received history. Voltaire showed that much of the teaching about the origins of Christianity and the foundation of the Church was clean contrary to common sense. He expected that the Roman Catholic faith would therefore cease to command belief. Conversely, when Paley wanted to prove the truth of the Christian religion, he faced the sceptic with a marshalled array of historical facts. Some were important, others trivial, but facts were facts to Paley—he might allow priority, but not exclusion. Again, d'Alembert, in his desire to wean people from old abuses, wished to destroy all historical records—if people did not know the past they could not cling to it. Yet the roots of Christianity depend for their main sustenance on something very different from historical facts, however important these may be. The achievements of Magna Carta rested upon a misunderstanding; those of the Social Contract theory on a myth.

The essential weakness of the encyclopædic teaching is epitomized in one of Diderot's " Pensées." " Égaré dans une forêt immense pendant la nuit," he says, " je n'ai qu'une petite lumière pour me conduire; survient un inconnu qui me dit : ' mon ami, souffle ta bougie pour mieux trouver ton chemin.' Cet inconnu est un théologien." The metaphor was unfortunate because, contrary to the rules of common sense, one candle on a dark night is less than no candle at all. Even if the metaphor may stand, Diderot's case falls to the ground because most people find their candle of reason a useless guide. The *Philosophes* could discredit the Church, but they could not replace it.

So even in France, which is said to be the most

rationalistic nation in Europe, and where the Encyclopædists did preach a new social evangel, the philosophy of common sense failed to do more than clear the way for a revolutionary, though in some ways retrogressive, creed.

This creed germinated in Rousseau's brain. Half-repellent, half-magnetic, he never ceased to be the strange, precocious and over-sensitive child who lives in the early pages of the *Confessions*—one of the strangest books ever written. Anything more opposed to the training and culture of those triumphant figures of the age, the English Whigs, it would be hard to imagine. In its pages the dignity of classic prose is superseded by an unrestrained though beautiful and vigorous style; the "easy assumption of effortless superiority" is abandoned for the candid relation of personal failings. Rousseau replaced reason on earth by imagination and sentiment; he dethroned her in heaven for an intimate and beneficent Supreme Being; his soul is not a blank film which records the impressions of the outside world through the lens of the five senses, but a creative artist which bends the material world to serve its own ideal. Though he was interested in many things, including bees and botany and the theory of music, his chief pleasure was to tramp the roads in freedom, not knowing where he would sleep nor how he would get his next meal, or to enjoy outdoor work and books with a friend among summer sights and sounds in the peace of the countryside. The pleasant feeling stirred in him by this way of life made him believe in God: " Je me levais tous les matins avant le soleil . . . tout en me promenant, je faisais ma prière, qui . . . consistait . . . dans une sincère élévation de cœur à l'auteur de cette aimable nature dont les beautés étaient sous mes yeux. Je n'ai jamais aimé à prier dans la chambre: il me semble que les murs . . . s'interposent entre Dieu et moi. J'aime à le contempler dans ses œuvres, tandis que mon cœur s'élève à lui."[1] Like the very different religious revivalists in England, he had his superstitions. The thought of Hell frightened him so much one day that he decided to put his fate in the next life to the arbitrament of chance. He was idly throwing stones at the time, and he made up his mind that if a certain stone hit a certain tree his soul would be saved; if it missed, he would go to Hell. But by choosing a tree, "fort gros et fort près,"[2] he insured himself against despair. With such a temperament Rousseau naturally hated the salon. Slow of thought, awkward in manner and cursed with a bad memory, yet as sensitive as he was vain, he both saw and resented his inability to shine at the conversational feasts of intellectual Paris. He led the great trek of those who were so much afraid of the drawing-room that they "took refuge in the nursery."[3] No wonder Hume quarrelled with him. No wonder the Encyclopædists hated and feared him. He started as a brilliant adherent of their cause, writing for the Encyclopædia, and corresponding with d'Alembert and Diderot. He lived on the borders of the same lake as Voltaire, tried to imitate his style,[4] and actually died in the same year. But as early as 1751 he alarmed d'Alembert by his *Discours sur les Sciences et les Arts*, in which he virtually claimed that knowledge of arts and sciences went hand in hand with the decline of human morality. After that, the breach steadily widened till Rousseau was the declared enemy of the Encyclopædists and possibly their victim. A measure of the gulf between them is suggested by the totally different impressions made on Voltaire and Rousseau by the same Swiss scenery. Instead of Voltaire's complacent appreciation of garden-flowers and select views and rural peace we begin to see through Rousseau's eyes the dancing lights

[1] *Confessions*, Bk. VI, Vol. II, p. 15.
[2] *Ib.*, Bk. VI, Vol. II, p. 24.
[3] Brandes, *Main Currents in Nineteenth Century Literature*, II, 174.   [4] *Confessions*, Bk. V, Vol. I, p. 257.

of purple, green and peacock in the water of the lake turned to dazzling sapphire by the wind, or the delicate blue of the larkspur above Montreux shining against the firs. Yet he cared no more than Voltaire to show us the dark gracious curves of the Jura facing the sharp whiteness of Mont Blanc, or the quick storm threaded with lightning, sweeping down from the mountains, blackening the lake, stripping the trees, then melting away as swiftly as it came. Nature never touched Rousseau's heart or pen with awe. In this at least he belonged to the eighteenth century.

He was true to the Renaissance tradition in other ways, too—in his desire to humanize the state, in disliking the tyranny of society and the Church, in believing in human nature and in the power of education. Nor could he wean himself from the eighteenth century longing for a new Lycurgus. But far more completely than Montesquieu, whose first influential disciple he was, he broke away from the heirs of the Renaissance and attacked their most cherished beliefs. For kings, philosophy and science he had small regard. He believed with Montesquieu in the empire of climate and circumstance. He changed the frigid deism of Voltaire into a warm emotional and individual faith. His belief in humanity was both warmer and colder than that of the Encyclopædists; warmer, because it did include " les cordonniers et les servantes "; colder, because it was not united to a belief in necessary and inevitable human progress. To say that Rousseau disbelieved in progress of any kind is scarcely true; if it were, he would hardly have been at pains to imagine an ideal polity, and to devise the means for making it; but he did not believe that humanity had progressed, nor that it would do so unless the discord were reconciled between the governing and the governed. The Encyclopædic effort to compass this by enlightened despotism he thought absurd, if only because kings are driven by their passions and interests like the rest of us.

Rousseau's expedient was to eliminate the distinction between rulers and people; the people ought to be their own rulers. "The words subject and sovereign," he says in the *Contrat Social*, "are identical correlatives, the idea of which meets in the single word 'citizen.'" For him the social compact, so far as it survived, became a declaration of the brotherhood of men.

In proclaiming the sovereignty of the ordinary man, Rousseau exalted in unmeasured terms the worth and dignity of each individual soul. This made him the patron saint of every kind of individualist. Yet he avoided the wilderness of isolated inhuman creatures where all extreme individualists ultimately lose themselves. He showed that a man can sustain his identity only by acting with other men; that he can find his soul only by losing it. He is equal to his fellows; all are sovereign; yet the will of each must bow before the general will. The "general will" is not the will of the majority, nor the sum total of all the individual wills in the state, but the transcendent will of the community in its corporate capacity. Whether such a thing as a "general will" exists may be disputed; how it can be expressed or recognized it is difficult to say, but it is clear that any support given to Rousseau's teaching on the subject would heighten the credit of the state and lower that of the individual. This is why Rousseau is also the patron saint of collectivists; and when in the nineteenth century nationalities were striving to become states, the indefinable but powerful force of nationalism seemed to be the "general will" and to justify Rousseau's idea, although the kind of state he had in mind was far more like his own Geneva, or the communes of France under the Girondists, than like Italy of the Risorgimento. How unsuccessful and inconsistent was the political machinery devised by Rousseau for a community of perfectly free and perfectly docile individuals, it was left for the Jacobins to prove by experience and for more peaceful generations to point out at leisure. At the time his ideas were symbols of an urgent faith. Wherever people fretted against the travesty of mediæval civilization which Voltaire had undermined, or against the materialistic culture he had praised, whether their quarrel was with churches, schools, governments or literary conventions, they all rallied to Rousseau's standard of revolt. This is as true of Germany as of France; in later days Mme. de Staël was to call Rousseau an "unconscious German."

German culture had followed a strange course. All through the first half of the eighteenth century Germans were busily copying the triumphant civilization which the French had inherited from the Renaissance. At Berlin they tried hardest and longest because Frederick the Great insisted, and he did not die till 1786. Moreover his enlightened despotism had done something to improve conditions of life in Prussia. But in most of the other German states, the encyclopædic ideal had failed. It did not induce the rulers to lessen social and economic restrictions, which were narrower and more petrified in parts of Germany than anywhere else in Europe. Instead, its aristocratic tendency merely fortified the petty tyranny of the princes. There was no great and varied future for an ambitious man unless he were a prince, no opening for genius, nothing but a drab parochial existence for anyone except on the stage.

About the middle of the century there began a quiet reaction against the borrowed French culture. A schoolmaster went to Rome to study classical times through classical remains, not through French conventions. His work was continued by Lessing (1729-1781) who made Europe laugh at the French classical tradition which approved the high heels and perukes still worn by French actors in the tragedies of Racine. Lessing was no less a rationalist than Voltaire or Diderot, no less a humanitarian than they. History to him, as to them, was a record of gradual enlightenment, and one of his greatest achievements was to free German culture from the control of theology. But he was too militant and independent to imitate. He was bold enough to assert that Shakespeare was a greater writer than Corneille, Racine, or Voltaire. He belonged rather to the creative days of the seventeenth century of which the Thirty Years War had deprived Germany of her fair share. Then came Herder (1744-1803). He, too, held some of the most cherished beliefs of the Encyclopædists. He believed that the world was made for humanity, that history was a record of progress, and he shared Montesquieu's belief in the moulding power of climate. But he, even more than Lessing, made it seem as if German culture were going backwards—leaving the conventionalism of eighteenth century France and even the intellectual Renaissance of the seventeenth century, and regaining the freshness and unconfined vision of Elizabethan England. He held that intuition was superior to reason; that genius and growth were more important than thought or action. His nationalism was not a mere reaction against French influence, but a positive faith symbolized in his rediscovery of the word " Volkslied." The philosophical revolt against eighteenth century ideas was led by Kant (1724-1804) and his disciple Fichte (1762-1814) who proclaimed the unconditioned sovereignty of spirit over matter, thus condemning the "sensational" teaching that had come down from Locke's psychology. Kant compared Rousseau's "discovery of the deep hidden nature of man" with the discoveries of Newton, implying that the one had done for morals what the other had done for physics.

But though German literature and philosophy and music were enriched at this time by some of the greatest geniuses the world has known, though just before the Revolution Germany was the most creative nation in the West, her culture could not escape from the conventionalism of France before it was caught up and whirled away by the dæmonic forces of the nineteenth century—democratic individualism and self-assertive nationalism.

The mixed ideals of the time are illustrated by Goethe's life (1749-1832). To begin with he was a crude nationalist and individualist. "Werther," who was inspired by his own experiences and Rousseau's *Nouvelle Héloïse*, is a passionate genius, tied half the day to his office, and confined for the rest to bourgeois society. What can he do but defy all rules and conventions? Yet in the end Goethe translated Voltaire's *Mahomet*. When he went to Assisi he never troubled to look at the wonderful mediæval Church of St. Francis, but spent all his time on a classical ruin. The older he grew, the more strictly he championed the regularity and correctness of late Renaissance art.

In this Schiller (1759-1805) was his ally. Other writers revolted against their conventional revival, but though German Hellenism, for instance, did aim to recapture the spirit rather than the form of Greek culture, though it freed itself from French influence, it was conventional in another way: it was no less German than Racine's plays are French.

Goethe himself could not live half-heartedly, he could not be Elizabethan and Voltairean at the same time, but his young admirers in Weimar led a double existence. "Werther" was their ideal, but though they indulged in unconventional pranks and loudly vaunted the right of heart and genius to be free of all control, they never lifted a finger to alter the social and political restraints which justified their discontent. In the minds of such vapourers the idealism of Kant degenerated to unphilosophical and childish dogma that was far enough removed from reason to condemn experimental science as utterly useless. This was to reject the best in Renaissance culture.

With all these cross-currents, the future of German civilization at the close of the eighteenth century was by no means clear. No one could be certain that the idealist and nationalist principles struggling for expression with a host of other aspirations would finally achieve a joint but discordant mastery which was largely due to the Revolution and Napoleon. All that could have been safely hazarded was this—that the civilization handed down from the Renaissance, set back for three generations by the Thirty Years War, but directing German culture through a great part of the eighteenth century, was now in the melting pot; that the civilization which emerged, however much it might owe to the Renaissance, would be fundamentally different.

As Voltaire and Montesquieu noticed, England was in some ways the country where Renaissance ideals had borne most fruit. The English, it is true, had achieved their strong state in defiance of Renaissance tradition. But they were comparatively tolerant both in politics and religion, their laws were not entirely inhuman, their economic restrictions were few, their social barriers less rigid than those of other nations. They had not only advanced human knowledge, but increased human comfort. And the general level of culture among their upper classes was high.

But unlike the French, the English made no attempt to broaden the basis of their enlightenment. English philosophy was no less exclusive than English culture, for thinkers like Bolingbroke or Hume had no desire to teach in the streets or even in the most respectable of shops. Yet it was in the eighteenth century that the shops and streets began to want a social and spiritual evangel. European civilization was beginning to be urban and industrial instead of rural and agricultural. The process was at first extremely slow, but in England it started first, and by the second half of the eighteenth century had become rapid. Great numbers of people were collecting in regions hitherto almost empty. The centres of population were moving from south and east to west and north. And before the century was out the mysterious and rapid increase of population had begun. There were a thousand needs to cater for, a thousand problems to be solved. But the leaders of society cared for none of these things, and the leaders of industry made use of them for their own ends.

The economic freedom, which the Encyclopædists and Physiocrats had demanded for France, and which was realized in England, may have been one reason why the English escaped from political revolution. But this does not mean that there was anything in common between the ideals of the French Revolution and the facts of the Industrial Revolution. On the contrary, the expansion of English industry and commerce, freed from restriction by Church or State or public opinion, produced a plutocratic civilization quite as exclusive and self-confident as that of the seventeenth century, and quite as undemocratic—a civilization of quality not quantity. But the nineteenth century quality was material not intellectual; the leaders of the nineteenth century triumphed in the acquisition of wealth, not of truth. This was hardly Condorcet's millennium.

If on the economic side Renaissance principles were condemned by success, they were condemned by a moral and spiritual failure which was more complete in England than in France. The English philosophers, whether wisely or not, made no attempt whatever to do the work that the Church had abandoned. Instead, the task of enlightening the people was suddenly shouldered by a single man. John Wesley reached the minds of large masses of people whom both Church and Renaissance had failed to touch. And his triumph, like Rousseau's, was the beginning of a new age and the death-knell of the old.

Wesley's (1703-1791) mission was to the uneducated

folk of large towns and growing villages. He said he desired no intercourse with "persons of quality," for "they do me no good, and I fear, I can do none to them."[1] But among the prisoners of Ludgate and Newgate, in the mining districts of Kingswood and Madeley, in large towns such as Bristol, Newcastle, Dublin and London itself, and in the villages of Cornwall and Northumbria, he and his friends created a spiritual kingdom which soon spread to North America.

Wesley claimed to live and die a member of the English Church in which he had been brought up, but both his teaching and organization were much influenced by the Moravian Brethren. He taught the need of personal conviction of "free, full and present salvation from all the guilt, all the power, and all the in-being of sin."[2] This personal conviction must be the accompaniment and result of a new spiritual birth, made necessary for all by the Fall of Man, and made possible, not by human merit, but by faith. After the New Birth, which was usually instantaneous, must come sanctification, or the slow, steady after-growth of holiness.

Thus the root-idea of Protestantism, the immediate and individual contact of the human soul with God, was reasserted. Argument and historical evidence were comparatively useless; the one essential was the conviction of God's speech with each man. God was thought of once more as the autocratic and omnipotent monarch who can do no wrong. Human life was seen as a battle-ground for a personal God and a personal Devil; every event as due to the direct intervention of the one or the other.

Methodism clearly had some bad results. Its converts were too apt to think God was using them as instruments whatever the folly they committed. When Wesley started to preach, some of his hearers

---

[1] Southey's *Life of Wesley* (World's Classics), p. 219.
[2] *Ib.*, p. 182.

would weep, writhe and fall down and groan aloud in spiritual torment. If Southey is to be credited, a Bristol maidservant who continued in a convulsion for fourteen hours was dismissed by her master, who said he " would have none in the house who had received the Holy Ghost."[1] When Wesley admitted that people were thrown into fits at his meetings, the Bishop of Bristol asked him to leave the diocese. Wesley refused to go, but though in his earlier years he seems to have thought these extravagances a sign of grace, he did not encourage them in later life, and they became rare. Other bad results of Methodism came from the adoption of some of the old Puritanical mistakes. Wesley's system of education, based on his belief that all amusement is at best a waste of time, was inhuman and foolish. He was strongly opposed not only to theatres, dancing and cards, but also to gay and rich clothing. " I pray let there be no costly silks among you, how grave so ever they may be ; . . . no Brussels lace ; no elephantine hats or bonnets— those scandals of female modesty." Worst of all, Methodism was intellectually narrow and sterile. Wesley lacked intellectual depth, and his movement produced no great thinkers. He himself believed in " possession " by evil spirits no less than in witchcraft. When his horse stumbled, he blamed the devil for it— not his own habit of reading on horseback. His immediate followers and his evangelical allies were hostile to the progress of science : " immorality and infidelity," said one of the latter, " spread their branches equally with human science."[2] With the exception of some fine hymns the literature they produced was negligible. Their sermons have as little permanent worth and interest as they are lengthy and numerous. " I sometimes preach half an hour

---

[1] *Ib.*, p. 211.
[2] Leslie Stephen, *English Thought in the Eighteenth Century*, Vol. II, 430.

before God comes," said one worthy, " and when He is come I can do no less than preach half an hour or three-quarters of an hour afterwards."[1] Wesley, however, preferred short sermons; he usually finished his own services within an hour.

Nevertheless, it was just because Wesley's appeal was moral and social and personal rather than intellectual that his success was phenomenal in village and colliery and slum. If his pictures of heaven and hell, God and the devil, conversion and damnation, were unphilosophical they were easy to understand, dramatic and alive. So far from being a hindrance, his superstitions and disbelief in modern scientific discovery probably helped him to approach people whose intellectual interests were more limited than his own. Moreover, in spite of a certain narrowness of outlook, and occasional intolerance of other people's views, he was in many ways extremely broad-minded. He put little stress on creeds, and great stress on a Christian way of life. He believed that virtuous Catholics and heretics and heathen were all capable of eternal life, and never required a confession of faith from those who wished to become Methodists. He did not even require them to leave their old communion. "The Presbyterian may be a Presbyterian still; the Independent or Anabaptist use his own method of worship; so may the Quaker, and none will contend with him about it. One condition, and one only is required,—a real desire to save their souls."[2]

Like St. Francis, Wesley wanted to show a new way of life, and not to found an " order "; like St. Francis, again, he adopted the forgotten rôle of a wandering preacher; but unlike St. Francis, whose life-work was preserved and perverted by another, he was able to organize his own movement on permanent and efficient lines. He could not only voice the opinions and divine

---

[1] Leslie Stephen, op. cit., Vol. II, 429.
[2] Southey, op. cit., p. 315.

the needs of a large class of people, but he had great legislative and administrative ability as well. In addition, his physical health and energy were extraordinary. He travelled thousands of miles in the year, into parts of England where " neither coach nor chaise had ever been seen." His first sermon was usually delivered at five o'clock in the morning, and it was not until after his eighty-sixth birthday that he " found it difficult to preach more than twice a day." He was thus able to inspect every part of his expanding kingdom, though to do so he had to travel in America, Scotland, Ireland, Wales and Holland, as well as in England, which he always regarded as having more claim on him than any other part of his world-parish.

But the most powerful lever of Methodism, more powerful than Wesley's doctrine or Whitefield's eloquence, than personality or organization, was the deep need for moral direction and spiritual comfort. This is illustrated by the poor success of the movement in Scotland. Wesley was disappointed that the hand of the Lord should tarry so long there, not seeing that Scotland was one of the few countries in Europe where religion was actively alive. Where it was dormant, as in England, or almost absent, as in some of the southern states of North America, Wesley carried all before him, and was helped rather than hindered by a persecution which seldom amounted to more than serious annoyance. Eighty years after his death his following numbered twelve million souls. In addition, the Wesleyans induced a parallel movement in the Anglican Church which they were finally forced to leave ; they were largely responsible not only for Methodism but for Evangelicalism.

A religion based on faith, easy to understand and full of emotional appeal, probably helped the English people, both for their good and for their ill, to live under social and economic conditions against which reason would have made them revolt. Meanwhile the better educated classes were finding scope for their imaginations in the sentimental books of Sterne and Richardson, in the unconventional and homely writings of Goldsmith, in the early fruits of a new outburst of lyric poetry. The literary conventions which the Age of Reason had supported, but which were never so deeply entrenched in England as in France, were being slowly ignored. As in Germany and France, heroes and heroines were no longer universally of noble blood. Nature began to seem spiritual and not material—to share in a mysterious way the life and faculties of men. So Wordsworth writes—

> ". . . the clouds were touched,
> And in their silent faces could be read
> Unutterable love . . ."

and listens to the "still, sad music of humanity." But the change, if steady, was slow; the English Romantic movement belonged to the nineteenth century. In England, as in Germany, it was the French Revolution that quickened the idealistic and imaginative impulses of literature, Napoleon who awakened the national spirit which slept beneath the cosmopolitanism of the eighteenth century.

In some ways it seems absurd to think of the Revolution as the final solvent of the humanistic civilization handed down from the Renaissance. The French Revolutionaries not only formulated the Rights of Man but fought for them. They achieved much of what Joseph II and Voltaire had worked for. They made and unmade constitutions in the name of reason, they divided France into artificial departments, they made the Church a lowly servant of the state, they relieved Protestants, actors and Jews from their civil disabilities, they ignored tradition and swept prejudice aside. For many years it was thought that the Revolution had sprung Minerva-like from the brain of the *Philosophes*: in the early years of the nineteenth century Barante was the only important writer to deny this. But he was right in asserting that intellectual propaganda is always the product rather than the creator of social conditions. It is indeed only when thinkers and prophets express the views of large masses of people that they seem to give direction to events. The *Philosophes* were respected and appealed to by the Revolutionaries, but this does not prove that they were responsible for the Revolution, nor that, on the whole, its achievements were such as they would have approved.

After the fall of the Girondists the spirit of the Revolution was anti-Voltairean even in theory. Rousseau's "Supreme Being" was Robespierre's God in heaven, Rousseau's tyrannical citizen-state Robespierre's ideal on earth. Condorcet, the aristocratic and extreme disciple of the Encyclopædists, lost his life for defending the king. Grimm, the educator of kings, fled from the Revolution which ruined him. Monarchy itself was condemned and the king and the queen destroyed. The commercial treaty with England came to an end in war. There was neither freedom of thought nor of speech in France, neither common sense nor humanity. The clergy who refused to accept the position assigned them by the "civil constitution" were persecuted with as much cruelty and intolerance as the Church had shown in Voltaire's day; the prisons were fuller than they had been under the *ancien régime*; justice was no less a travesty. Savage executions at home were followed by bloodshed and forcible propaganda abroad. In short, the dearest wishes of the *Philosophes* were reversed; there was democratic tyranny for benevolent autocracy, cruelty for kindness, prejudice for reason, war for peace.

Napoleon with his Code, with his mechanical and efficient administrative system, his encouragement of industry and science, his interest in education, his patronage of art and letters, in many ways resembled the Benevolent Despots. But he stifled free thought and restored the Catholic religion. His empire was too narrow to hold both himself and Madame de Staël.

When reaction followed, the *Philosophes* were discredited still more. By a common irony their repute was injured by one of those false beliefs whose power they had despised, but which so often prevail over fact. Though their responsibility for the Revolution was small, though they would bitterly have condemned its words and acts, the whole movement was fathered upon them, and their names accordingly reviled. French literature of the early nineteenth century was thus further from the Renaissance tradition than was the contemporary literature of Germany and England ; it was soaked in Roman Catholicism, in deference to authority, in spurious mediævalism, in sentimental horror of reason and science—in everything that the *Philosophes* most despised and condemned. According to de Maistre, the Pope and the public executioner were the noblest pillars of society. Chateaubriand was horror-struck when he heard a child answer the question "What is a man?" with the degrading word "a mammal." He promised to go to the Holy Land " with the ideas, aims and feelings of a mediæval pilgrim,"[1] and he brought back water from the Jordan.

Even when the excesses of Revolution and Reaction had passed, the main ideas inherited from the Revolution by nineteenth century Europe were unlike the ideas that had animated the chief writers and thinkers of the Renaissance tradition. Ideas, it is true, never die. Greece insurgent against the Ottoman Empire, Shelley in revolt against convention, were descended from Machiavelli's independent state, Luther's independent man. But the nineteenth century faith in man and the state had little in common with the teaching of Descartes or Bacon, of Hobbes or Voltaire.

[1] Brandes, op. cit., Vol. III, 142.

CONCLUSION

In the nineteenth century the heir of the Revolution demanded political liberty for the individual. Little by little, the old qualifications for rulership were abandoned. Democrats thought it better to have no culture rather than one that could not be shared by all. And individualism, thus broadened, lost both advocates and pride. Man was no longer the lonely but confident pigmy challenging the huge indifferent universe with his reason, but the humble child of nature, God or circumstance, gratefully idealistic or impotently rebellious as the case might be. Experience taught that individualism was a will-o'-the-wisp for all save the powerful or rich; the poor and weak must fight in groups. The duty of the state was no longer to give free play to individuals, but, in the interests of the many, to control the few. The state itself was thought of, not as an efficient machine controlled by a master-mechanic whose only title was his skill, but as the visible and active body of a hidden spirit, sovereign not by virtue of utility, but of the national spirit which it expressed. Poland was a disembodied spirit because its nationality had no state; the non-national state of Austria was an unrighteous anomaly. Metternich took care to uphold the eighteenth century political system as long as he could, but he stood for the past and not for the future. The Renaissance tradition had lost its youth and its creativeness: it persuaded the elderly to keep what they could of the past; it no longer encouraged the young to create a new world and to sweep away the old.

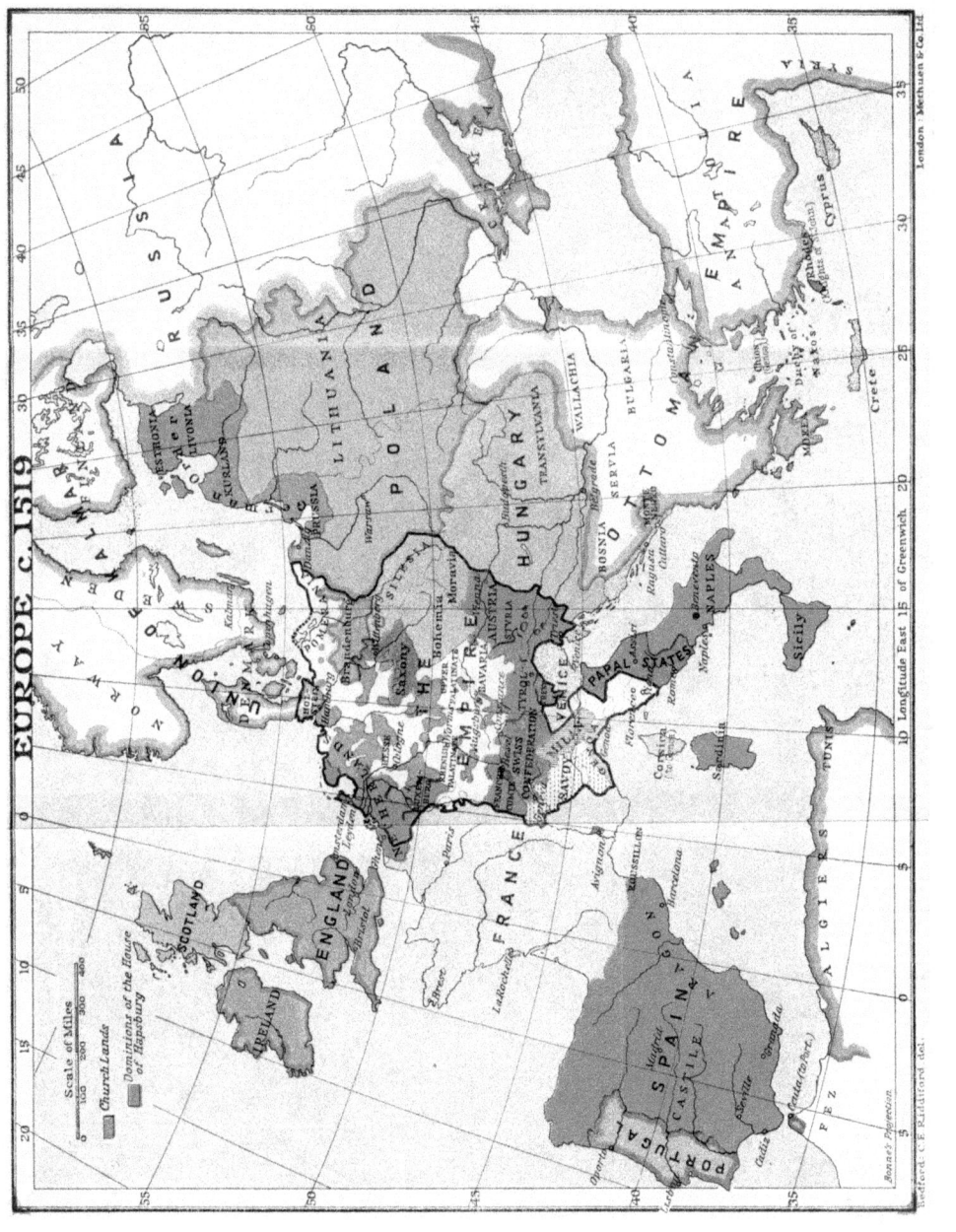

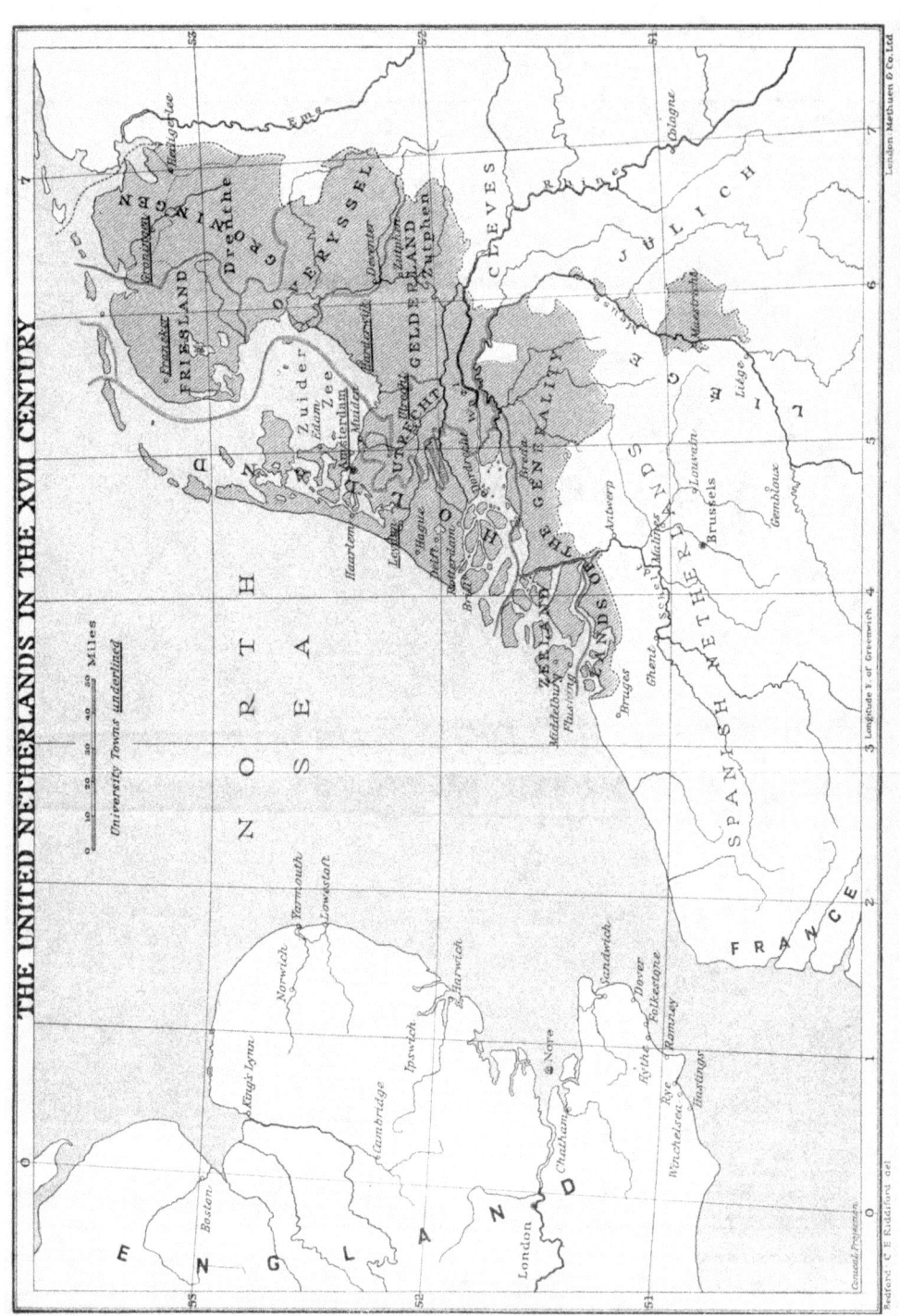

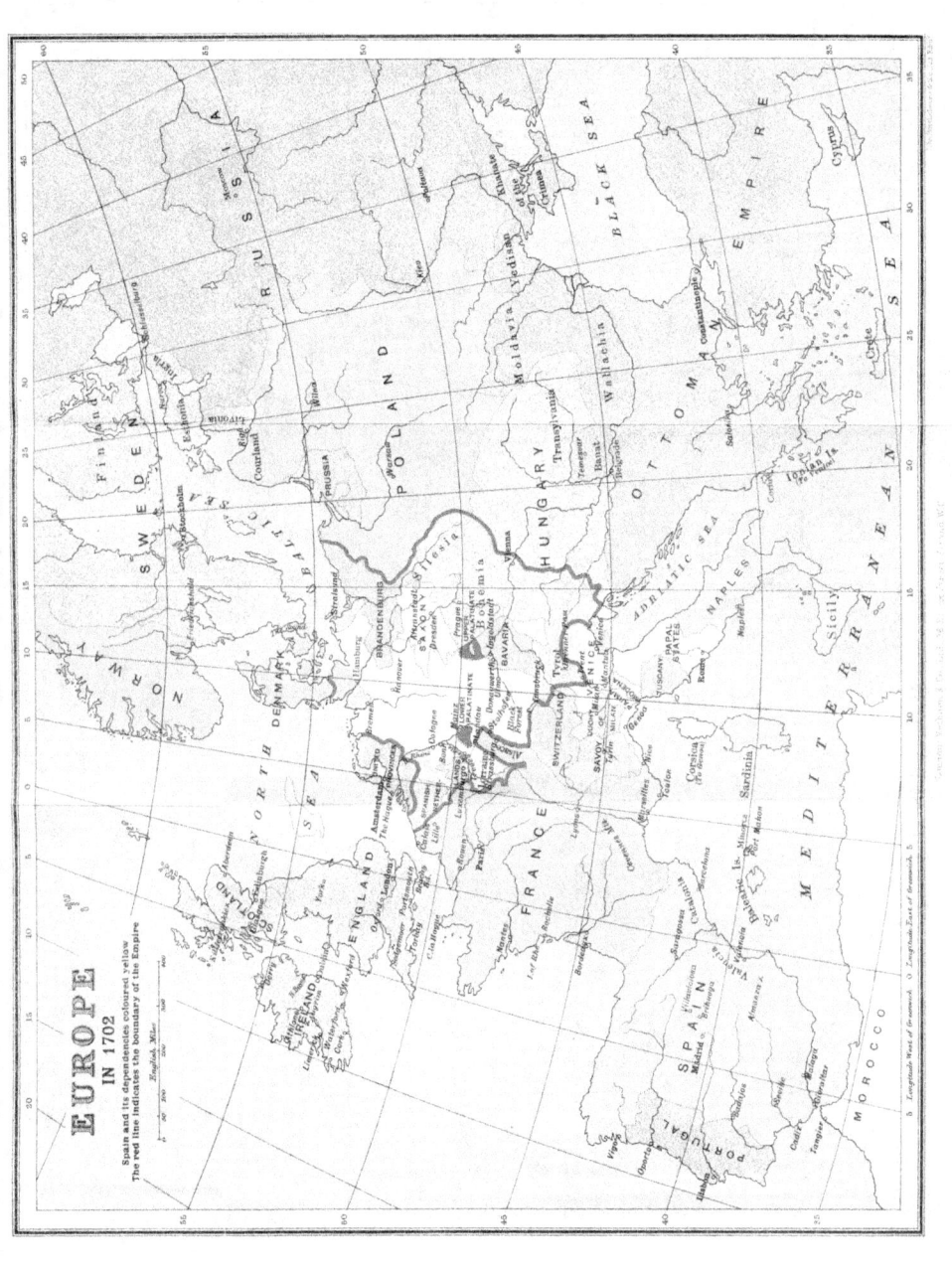

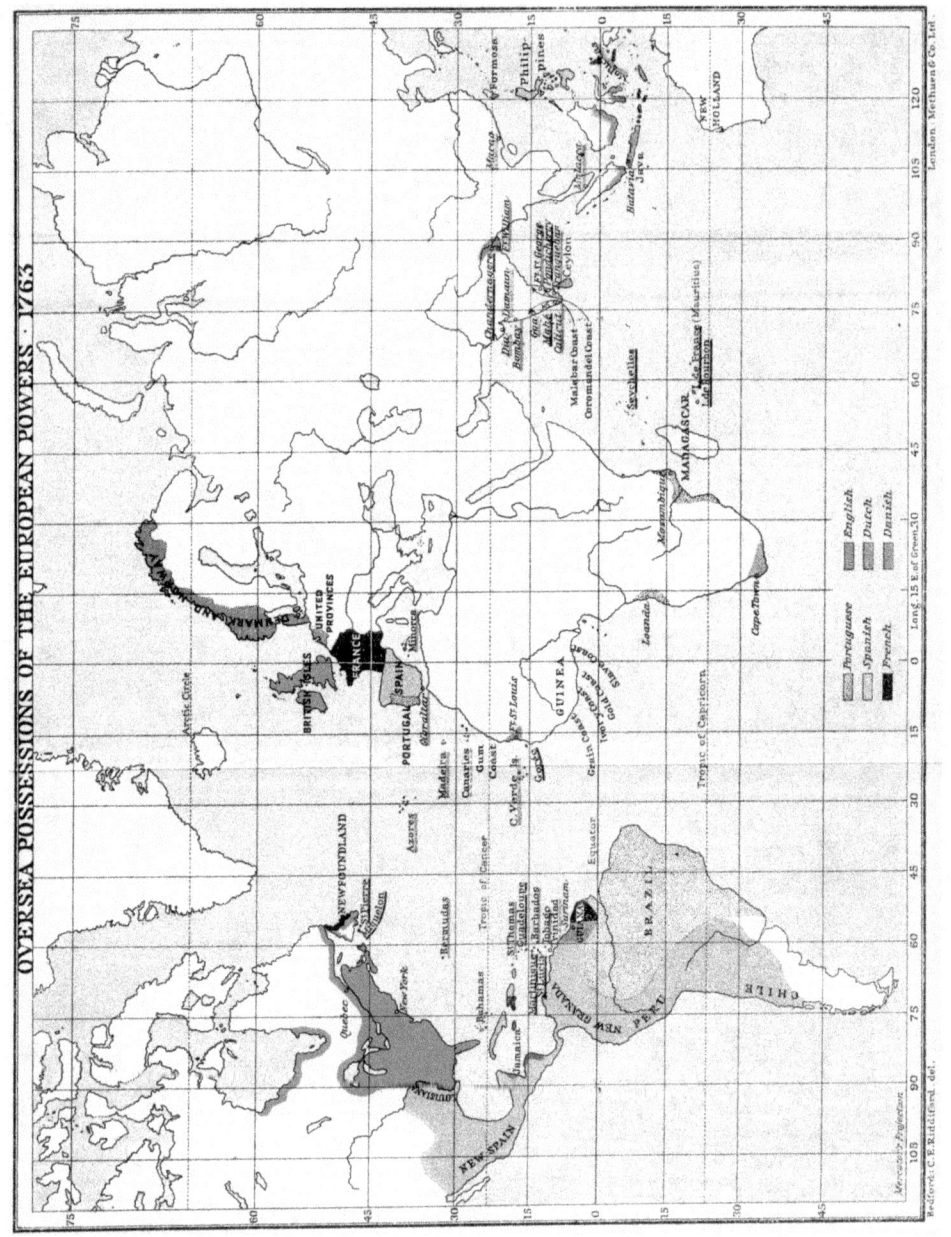

INDEX

America—
  discovery of, 13
  colonization of, 109 seqq
  toleration in, 97–8
American Revolution, 177–8
Aristotle, 3, 81, 101

Bacon, Francis, 12, 21, 99, 102, 105–6, 130, 145

Calvin, John, 40–1, 51
Calvinists, 41, 51, 57, 96
Catharine II of Russia, 108, 141, 153, 155 157 seqq.
Child, Sir Josiah, 71–3, 81
Colbert, 63–4, 70
Colonization, Chapter V *passim*, 63, 97, 129
Conciliar Movement, 28–30
Council of Trent, 43–4
Counter-Reformation, 42–9
Cromwell, 87, 95, 96

D'Alembert, 130, 134, 137, 141, 144, 145, 182
Descartes, 102–4, 106, 130, 133
De St. Pierre, 132, 133, 134, 136, 138, 139, 142, 176
Diderot, 132, 137 seqq., 144–50, 153, 164, 166, 180–1, 182, 187

Encyclopædia, the, 130, 141–4, 150, 179–80, 184
Erasmus, 5, 33–6, 139
Evelyn, John, 60, 67, 69, 75, 105

Francis, St., 7, 8, 27, 28, 181, 194
Frederick the Great, 108, 153, 155, 157 seqq., 175, 181

Goethe, 189
Greek. *See* Revival of Learning, 34
  writers, knowledge of, in Middle Ages, 3–4
  writers, influence of, in seventeenth century, 86, 87, 100
Grotius, 67, 81, 92–3, 94

Henry IV of France, 53–4, 63
Hobbes, Thomas, 52, 81, 85–6, 89, 94, 101, 106
Holy Roman Empire, 15, 20, 24, 29, 36, 37, 52, 91, 92, 93–4

International Law, development of, 90–4

Jansenists, 57, 58, 104, 144
Jesuits, 46–8, 55, 57, 97, 104, 109, 144
Joseph II, 141, 155, 158–9, 163–5, 166, 167, 168, 176, 196

Locke, John, 90, 98, 129
Louis XIV, 49, 54, 56 seqq., 76, 77, 78, 88, 94, 130, 176
Luther, 8, 23, 36–40, 43, 51–2, 96
Lutherans, the, 40, 41, 42, 51

Machiavelli, 9, 11, 18 *seqq.*, 52, 92-3, 106
Mercantilism, 61-5, 70, 122 *seqq.*, 161-3
Middle Ages—
  classical knowledge in, 2, 3
  Bible in, 5
  art in, 6, 7
  political ideals of, 15, 19
  loss of civilization of, 24, 25
  theology in, 34, 69, 100-1
  institutions of, their survival in modern Europe, 131, 162
  and French literature in early nineteenth century, 198
Milton, 80, 81, 90, 99, 104
Monarchy, in France, England and Spain, 16
  economic and political foundations of, 17
  and Renaissance, 17, 18
  and Reformation, 48, 49, 52
  hostile to Church, 56, 58-9, 88, 158
  hostile to individual liberty, 23, 51, 57, 59, 130
  challenged by—
    Calvinists and Presbyterians, 51
    Huguenots, 53, 55
    Holland, 68, 76
    study of classics, 86
    Puritans, 87
    Social Contract theory, 89
    theory of natural law, 91
    Jesuits and Independents, 97
    Rousseau, 185
  supported by—
    Machiavelli, 20, 23
    Luther, 23, 37, 52
    Richelieu, 54-6
    Hobbes, 86, 89-90
    Grotius, 93
    the *Philosophes*, 153-4
  in seventeenth century France, 52-65
  in seventeenth century England, 76, 87 *seqq.*, 105
  of France copied by other states, 49, 65, Chapter VII *passim*

Monarchy—
  expands overseas, Chapter V *passim*
Montesquieu, 132, 136, 137-9, 140, 143, 185, 190

Natural Law, 90-3, 94-5
Newton, Sir Isaac, 99, 105

Papacy—
  and Renaissance, 15, 30, 31
  and New Monarchies, 16, 17, 43
  and reform, 26, 27, 30-3
  and Franciscan movement, 27-8
  and Conciliar movement, 28-30
  and Counter - Reformation, 44-6
  and Louis XIV, 56-9
  discredited, 91, 92
  at Westphalia, 93
  and Joseph II, 159
  and de Maistre, 198
Philosophes, the—
  beliefs of, 130-6, 153-4, 176-7
  aims of, 136-7, 139
  methods of, 140-1, 151, 152-3, 165-6
  failure of, 177, 180-3
  and French Revolution, 196-8
Physiocrats, the, 150-1, 154, 161, 162, 191
Press, 4, 33, 59, 165, 171, 172
Puritans, the, 87, 88, 95, 96, 97, 105

Racine, 79, 80, 81, 82-4, 85, 137
Reformation, Chapter II *passim*
  and individual liberty, 51, 96
  and pessimism, 106
Renaissance—
  of classical learning. *See* Revival of Learning
  and humanism, 6-8, 106
  and Church, 6, 31-3
  emphasizes national differences, 8-11

INDEX

Renaissance—
  geographical discoveries of, and their effects, 11-14, Chapter V *passim*
  stimulates trade, 13-14
  patrons of, 14-15
  stimulates despotism, 15, 17-23, 50-2
  and Papacy, 15, 30, 45
  stimulates individualism, 33
  benefits the few, not the many, 23-4, 179
  results in loss of mediæval ideals, 24-5
  gives driving-force to Reformation, 31-3, 36
  scholarship and Jesuits, 47
  in seventeenth century Holland, 67-9
  triumph of, in seventeenth century, 77, 106-7
  loses breadth, 79
  literature of, 9, 79-85
  produces revolution in methods of thought, 99-107
  attempt to complete work of, in eighteenth century, Chapter VI *passim*
  Montesquieu and traditions of, 138
  culminates in French philosophy of eighteenth century, 130, 153, 176-7
  Diderot's descent from, 144
  failure of main ideas of, 149, 177, 180, 191, 199
  and benevolent despotism, 156
  Heirs of, in eighteenth century England, 174
  Political theory of, never true to facts, 176

Renaissance—
  Rousseau and traditions of, 185
  Traditions of—
    in Germany, 187-9
    and French Revolution, 196-7
    and Napoleon, 197-8
Revival of Learning, 1-6, 18, 79, 85, 89, 91, 99
Revolution, French, 25, 178, 190, 191, 196-7, 198
Richelieu, 54-6
Roman Empire, 2, 18, 85
Roman Law, 18, 85, 90, 92
Roman Republic, 2, 18, 85
Rousseau, Jean-Jacques, 142, 145, 149, 173, 181, 183-7, 189

Social Contract, theory of, 89-90, 182, 186

Toleration, religious, 95 *seqq.*, 152, 159, 172
Turgot, 142, 161

Vinci, Leonardo da, 8, 10, 11, 78, 144
Voltaire, 132 *seqq.*, 145, 146, 147, 151-2, 153, 171, 173, 180, 182, 184, 185, 187, 190, 196, 197

Wesley, John, 172, 191-5
Westphalia, Peace of, 65, 93
Whigs, the, 88, 90, 98, 150, 171, 173-5, 179, 183

For Product Safety Concerns and Information please contact our EU representative GPSR@taylorandfrancis.com
Taylor & Francis Verlag GmbH, Kaufingerstraße 24, 80331 München, Germany

www.ingramcontent.com/pod-product-compliance
Lightning Source LLC
Chambersburg PA
CBHW062225300426
44115CB00012BA/2231